Dear Juniors,

This handbook is especially for you. It will tell you about handling your dog and how to compete in Junior Showmanship. There are lessons for you to follow and helpful hints to guide you.

You will learn how Junior Showmanship began and how it has changed. In the Junior Hall of Fame you will see the champion handlers of Junior Showmanship over the years. How to begin a junior club and a complete program guide for clubs are included. Careers for junior graduates are discussed. You will also find a special place to keep your own records and notes. Every subject is illustrated with photographs and drawings.

We hope that this book will help you become a better handler and a more knowledgeable dog fancier.

Your friends,

Marsha and Bethny

P.S. Tell your parents there's a chapter for them too!

The

JUNIOR SHOWMANSHIP HANDBOOK

Marsha and Bethny with two Setters under judge Howard C. Smith.

The JUNIOR SHOWMANSHIP HANDBOOK

by
MARSHA HALL BROWN
BETHNY HALL MASON
Illustrated

A complete book of instruction on
HOW TO BEGIN
HOW TO HANDLE
and HOW TO WIN
in Junior Showmanship competition at dog shows.

1971
HOWELL BOOK HOUSE Inc.
845 Third Avenue
New York, N.Y. 10022

To

THOMAS WATKINS HALL
and
FLORENCE FARRIER HALL

for *his* perseverance and dedication;
for *her* patience and understanding;
for *their* example of sportsmanship,
hard work and zest for living.

Contents

	Acknowledgments	9
	Foreword	11
1.	The Story of Junior Showmanship	15
2.	How to Begin in Junior Showmanship	18
3.	How to Look Like a Winner	27
4.	How to Handle in Junior Showmanship	31
5.	How to Win in Junior Showmanship	56
6.	Let's Play Twenty Questions	74
7.	Particularly for Parents	79
8.	You Can Be a Six-Star Junior	83
9.	Looking Ahead—Careers for You	87
10.	Junior "Hall of Fame"	99
11.	Junior Crowns	118
	Westminster Winners	122
	AKC Regulations for Junior Showmanship	123

All drawings are by the authors.

BEST DOG
IN SHOW

The youngest handler to ever score an all-breed Best
in Show in American Kennel Club history—Laura
Meisels, eight years old, of Houston, Texas. At the
Calcasieu KC show at Lake Charles, La. on April 17,
1971, Laura guided her West Highland White Terrier,
White Oaks Lover Boy, from the classes to win of the
Group under judge Maxwell Riddle, and on to the
pictured win of Best in Show under judge Vance H.
Evans. Entry was nearly 700 dogs. Laura finished Lover
Boy to championship in four shows. In her one time
in Junior Showmanship competition, at Houston in
March 1971 before the present 10-year-old minimum
was in effect, Laura was Best Junior Handler in Show.

Acknowledgments

TO Cynthia Dody, Elizabeth Brown, Douglas Le Porte, Barbara Le Porte, Bethny Brown, Kimberly Haigler, Dale Hughes, Sue Hanson, Cindy Hanson, Jeffrey Silverman, and Rebecca Mason, our thanks for their patience in front of our cameras.

Leonard Brumby, Jr., Mrs. William H. Long, Jr., Elsworth S. Howell, Thomas Yahn, and the American Kennel Club made it possible for us to write the history of Junior Showmanship.

We appreciate the help given by M. Christine Sidler, D.V.M., in the preparation of the article on Veterinary Medicine as a career, in Chapter 9.

Our thanks to *Popular Dogs* for permission to reprint "You Can Be A Six-Star Junior" (Page 83), which first appeared in that magazine as an article by Marsha Hall Brown.

We thank, too, our husbands—Bob and Ray, for living with this book and its authors.

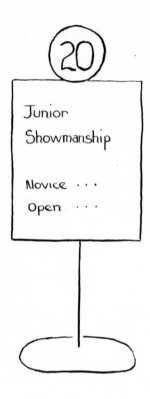

Foreword

IT has been my privilege to know the charming young authors of this book for more than twenty years, and they were *very* young indeed when I first met them and their family.

Marsha Hall Brown and Bethny Hall Mason typify the all-American girl in the finest meaning of the term. The versatility of their interests and of their achievements was—and remains—remarkable. In dogs and in other activities their careers are almost parallel.

Marsha began showing dogs when she was only nine years old and finished her first champion when she was 15. She won ten Children's Handling and Junior Showmanship first prizes. In 1955 she won the Gaines Youth Award for the Girl Show Dog Fancier of the Year. She has handled a good number of her family's English Setters to championships, Bests of Breed and Sporting Group wins. She has also handled Irish and Gordon Setters, Beagles, Bassetts and Collies.

For ten years Marsha has written an outstanding column on Junior Showmanship for *Popular Dogs* magazine. She was a licensed professional handler for three years and since 1967 has served as a licensed American Kennel Club judge. She has contributed much to dog clubs, serving as Vice President of the English Setter Association of America for five years and is a founding member of the Hudson English Setter Club. Presently she is a member of the California English Setter Club and of the English Setter Association of America.

Marsha has achieved success in other fields as well. As a high school student, she was editor of the year book of the Rhode Island Honor Society. Training in the National Red Cross Aquatic School, she became Director of Swimming and

Water Safety for the town of Smithfield, Maine; indeed she spent 25 years in Girl Scouting, was a Brownie leader and has worked actively for the Red Cross.

Her sister, Bethny, has also accomplished high honors in a variety of activities. In high school she was President of the Girls Athletic Association, was also a member of the Rhode Island Honor Society, and won the Spartan medal, an annual award to the writer of the best essay. Bethny, too, has been active in the Red Cross, particularly in its Aquatic School. She was swimming instructor for the town of North Providence, Rhode Island and held the same position for the Girl Scouts of Rhode Island.

Bethny showed her first dog at a sanction match at the tender age of 4 years. She finished her first champion when only 11 and in all, guided ten dogs to their American Kennel Club championships. In addition to English Setters, she has handled Irish and Gordon Setters, Pointers, Afghans, Beagles and Schipperkes. She joined her sister as columnist for *Popular Dogs*. Recently she was appointed Junior Advisor of the English Setter Club of New England.

Bethny's record in Junior Showmanship may never be equalled. She won a total of 81 Firsts in the Open Class of that competition. For the years 1956, 1957, and 1958, she won the Stewards' Club of America award as the National Girl Show Handler of the Year. For three consecutive years she was the Champion Junior Handler of both the English Setter Club of New England and the English Setter Association of America. In 1958 Governor Ribicoff of Connecticut presented her with the Best Junior Handler trophy awarded annually by that state's governor. In 1959 she duplicated her sister's achievement by winning the Gaines award as Girl Show Dog Fancier of the Year. Her record at the prestigious Westminster Kennel Club Junior Showmanship competition was incredible—in 1956 and 1957 she won third place at this event, and in 1959 won its top award, retiring from Junior Showmanship at only 13 years of age.

Though married, and raising their own Junior Showmen, Marsha and Bethny continue to serve dogs and dog lovers. In this book they present to current and future participants in Junior Showmanship their incomparable guidance and advice based on their own inimitable efforts and crowning successes. It is an honor and rare privilege for Howell Book House to publish The Junior Showmanship Handbook written by two such outstanding and remarkable all-American girls.

—ELSWORTH S. HOWELL

Rebecca Mason, Bethny's daughter.

Leonard Brumby, Sr.

George F. Foley

The founders of Junior Showmanship

1/The Story of
Junior Showmanship

IN the late 1920s, some active dog fanciers became interested in encouraging the participation of young people at the dog shows. These fanciers were mainly from the Long Island and Westchester areas of New York, and from southern Connecticut. They believed that the future of the dog world depended upon the interest and activities of the youth of the present.

Leonard Brumby, Sr., Founder

Leonard Brumby, Sr., was a well-known professional handler, and a member and officer of the Westbury Kennel Club. He worked hard to convince members and other exhibitors that it was important for children to take an active part in dog shows. Mr. Brumby felt that the children should have their own competition. He suggested that a competition based on handling ability would be particularly helpful and interesting for them. As a result of his efforts, the first Children's Handling Class was held at the Westbury Kennel Club show, Long Island, N.Y. in 1932.

Candy for All

The first classes for Children's Handling were listed in the Westbury premium list (the announcement that is sent out in advance of each show to let exhibitors know what prizes are being offered) as follows:
    Class A—Boys under 14 years.
    Class B—Girls under 14 years.

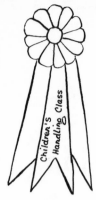

In 1933, the Westbury club offered Children's Handling for boys and girls under 15 years of age, and another class for boys and girls under 10 years of age. "Candy for all, but no unruly dogs," was announced in the premium list.

George F. Foley, who was superintendent of many of the large shows at the time, took an active interest in the Children's Handling classes. He encouraged the show-giving clubs to include a competition for young people. Soon there were Children's Handling classes at many of the dog shows in the East.

Westminster Competition

In 1933, the first Children's Handling Championship was held at the Westminster Kennel Club show at Madison Square Garden in New York City. Boys and girls who had won a first place in Children's Handling during the year were eligible to compete. However, juniors who scored three first place wins were barred from further competition until after the Westminster finals. The winner of the Handling Championship was presented with the Grand Challenge Trophy.

The Memorial Trophy

In 1949, the Professional Handlers' Association presented the Westminster Children's Handling Champion with a new trophy. The Leonard Brumby Sr. Memorial Trophy became the most famous junior award. Given in honor and memory of the founder of Children's Handling, the trophy is still awarded annually.

Changes and More Changes

The name of the competition was changed from Children's Handling to Junior Showmanship in 1951.

Children's Handling had begun with a handful of boys and girls in the New York area, and had grown to be a popular sport in which thousands of young people, throughout the United States and Canada, participated. What had originally been just a novel contest for children and their dogs became a highly competitive and sophisticated competition.

Changes developed in the selection of judges and in judging procedures. In the early years, there were no special qualifications required of Children's Handling judges. Celebrities and movie stars were often invited to judge, and their choice of a winner was not always based on skillful handling. Boys and girls were sometimes requested to exchange dogs with others in the class. The Professional Handlers Association acted to correct this situation by encouraging its members to judge more often, and soon only licensed handlers were allowed to preside.

There were changes in the class divisions, too. The Children's Handling classes were usually divided into a class for boys, and a class for girls. Large shows sometimes provided two classes for each, with an age division. Soon after the competition became Junior Showmanship, however, the classes were opened to either boys or girls, and divided by age only.

Further major changes were introduced in the mid-1950s. A class for novice juniors was offered, and experienced juniors were provided with open competition. As the popularity of Junior Showmanship grew, these Novice and Open classes were divided by age.

The growth of Junior Showmanship had thus made necessary many changes, but there was still one step to go. Competition was not uniform across the country. Each area had different age requirements and different classes. Some areas did not hold classes for Westminster eligibility.

Finally, in 1971, Junior Showmanship achieved full status. The American Kennel Club announced its official recognition of the competition. Rules and regulations were standardized. Junior Showmanship has become an important part of every dog show.

17

2/How to Begin in Junior Showmanship

HI! Welcome to the world of Junior Showmanship. Beginning this new adventure with your dog will be fun. It will be interesting. It will be exciting. You will meet many interesting people and you will make new friends. So, let's not wait any longer — let's begin.

Be An Observer

Go to several shows as a visitor. Watch the competition in the breed you will be handling.

Notice that each class that enters the ring is judged in a similar way. The judge motions for all dogs to trot (or gait) around the ring. He then examines each dog individually. First he examines the dog in a standing or show pose position. Then he watches the dog in motion. After he has judged all the dogs in the ring and made his decision, he sends the chosen dogs to the place markers in the ring and awards the ribbons to the handlers.

Observe the people who are handling in the ring. How do they gait the dog? How do they pose the dog? How do they handle the lead? (In dog shows, the leash is usually called the lead — you lead your dog into the ring. In this book, we will use the word *lead*.)

Now go to the Junior Showmanship ring and watch the classes carefully. Note that the fine points of the dog are not being considered here. THE JUNIORS ARE JUDGED ONLY ON THEIR ABILITY TO HANDLE. Because it is handling abilities rather than dogs that are being judged, the Junior Showmanship classes often take longer to judge.

The three basic handling skills will be required for Junior Showmanship: juniors will gait their dogs together around the ring, will pose their dogs for examination, and will gait their dogs individually. Juniors are also tested on other handling skills, such as gaiting in a certain pattern, posing the dog in a line parallel (side by side) to other dogs, or being required with another junior to gait their dogs at the same time.

Learn the Rules

Look in the show catalog for the rules and classes offered for Junior Showmanship at the show. Age requirements and the number and type of classes may differ at shows. Most shows use the following competition announcement:

> Novice A: For Boys and Girls, 10 to 12 years inclusive, who have never won a Junior Showmanship competition.
> Novice B: For Boys and Girls, 13 to 16 years inclusive, who have never won a Junior Showmanship competition.
> Open C: For Boys and Girls, 10 to 12 years inclusive, who have won one or more Junior Showmanship competitions.
> Open D: For Boys and Girls, 13 to 16 years inclusive, who have won one or more Junior Showmanship competitions.

Each dog handled in a regular Junior Showmanship class must be entered and shown in one of the breed or Obedience classes at the show, or must be entered for Junior Showmanship only. Each dog must be owned or co-owned by the junior handler, or by the junior handler's father, mother, brother, sister, uncle, aunt, grandfather or grandmother, including the corresponding step and half relations. Every dog entered for Junior Showmanship must be eligible to compete in dog shows or Obedience trials. At a specialty show, each dog must be of the breed for which the show is held.

A dog that has been excused or disqualified by a breed judge or by a Bench Show Committee may still be handled in Junior Showmanship if eligible to compete in Obedience trials. However, a dog that has been rejected, dismissed or excused by the veterinarian for the protection of the other dogs at the show, or for the protection of the dog excused, may not be handled in Junior Showmanship.

19

Prizes shall be awarded for skillful handling only, merit of the dog not to count.

Only First Place in the Open Divisions will count toward winning eligibility to compete for the Leonard Brumby, Sr. Memorial Trophy each year at the Westminster Kennel Club show, Madison Square Garden, N.Y. in February.

A Helping Hand

Seek the help of someone who handles your breed and knows the correct ways to pose and gait this breed.

The breed association or club may have a member in charge of junior activities or they may suggest a member who will help you. A breeder who handles and is familiar with proper handling skills may be helpful. A professional handler who has had experience with your breed may also be helpful. Remember: each breed is handled in a particular way. It is necessary that you learn the proper way to handle your breed.

Ready, Set, Handle!

Now it is time to take the lead in your hand. At home, find a place to practice. This can be in your yard, at a nearby park, or an unused area of a parking lot or school yard. In winter weather your practice space may be a garage or basement. If possible, set up a practice ring with five stakes and twine or yarn. Or use five bricks or similar objects to mark off the area you will use for a temporary ring. Chalk can also be used to mark a temporary ring on pavement.

Exercise your dog for several minutes before you begin the practice session. It is important that your dog be comfortable and calm before each lesson.

Now place the show lead on your dog. The lead should be high on the neck and under the throat so that you have complete control of the dog.

Hold the lead in your left hand. Extend your left arm out from your shoulder so that your arm is parallel to the ground. Gather all the extra lead inside your hand. Secure your grasp on the lead by looping the first inch of lead which shows (next to your hand), over your index finger and under your remaining fingers.

21

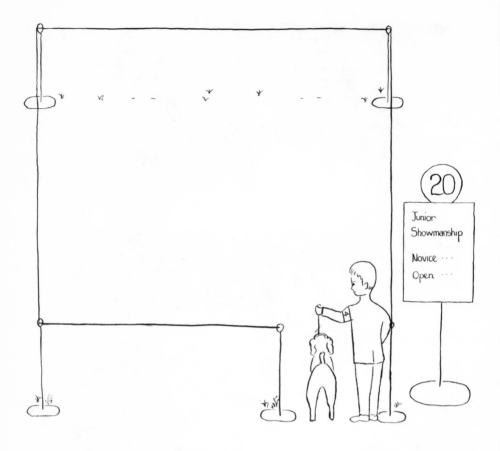

Enter the practice ring with your dog on your left and the show lead in your left hand. Turn right and walk all the way around the inside of the ring. **Ring traffic always travels counter-clockwise.** Now that you know the route, go around the ring again. Move at a speed which allows your dog to trot easily at your side.

Bring your dog to a stop. Place your dog in a show pose. Remember how the dogs looked at the show in the breed class? Remember how the handlers carefully placed the feet and held the dog in a pose? Is your dog posed correctly for its

22

breed? Are you holding the head and tail or lead and tail in the proper way? Do you have control over your dog?

Get ready to gait. Place the lead high on the neck and hold the lead in the left hand. Begin at one side of the ring and walk in a straight line across the ring and STOP.

Do not move from your gaiting position. Is your left arm extended shoulder height? Is your dog on your left?

Extend your free hand (right hand) across in front of you and reach for your left hand. (Do not move your body or feet.) Transfer the lead coil from your left hand into your right hand. Place your left hand at your side and turn toward that hand until you are facing the direction of return. Walk back across the ring in a straight line.

This time, your dog will be on your right side. Your right arm is extended out and you are holding the lead in your right hand. Now repeat this straight-line gaiting exercise several times moving your dog at the proper speed.

You have now performed the three basic handling skills: gaiting in a circle, posing your dog, and gaiting in a straight line. You have also learned how to enter the ring, how to hold the lead securely, and how to change hands and direction.

24

Make this fun for your dog. Keep this practice session short. Plan ten minutes for the adult dog and half that time for a puppy. Regular daily practice is important for you and your dog. Two long sessions twice a week should not be substituted for daily practice. Praise your dog often at practice time. Reward your dog at the end of each session with a cheerful voice and a short playtime. Remember: learn to control, train and handle your dog, but do it with a gentle hand and a kind heart.

Sanctioned matches are for you. A match is a practice show which is sanctioned by the American Kennel Club. Many breed clubs and all-breed clubs hold these informal shows during the year. Most matches offer breed, Obedience and Junior Showmanship classes. If possible make your debut at a local match show. You may get extra practice there by handling your dog in in the breed classes, as well as in Junior Showmanship.

Your first competition in Junior Showmanship is a big adventure. Whether it is at a match show or a regular point show (in which championship points are awarded) three helpful hints will speed you to early success:
1. Watch the other Junior Showmanship Classes.
2. When the judge is through, ask for corrective criticism.
3. Remember your dog—pat him and praise him. You couldn't have competed without him.

The Winning
Look

3/How to Look Like A Winner

YOUR whole appearance is just as important as the way you handle. Your clothes, grooming and manners can make you look like a winner. Always be well groomed. Choose clothes which are appropriate for a sporting event and comfortable to work in. Make sure they are clean, neat, and pressed.

Be courteous to the judge and to other handlers. Be especially considerate toward juniors who are just beginning. Be a good sport. Congratulate the winner before you leave the ring. Don't get upset if you are not the judge's choice today.

Leave your emotions at home.

For Boys

The winning look for boys should include a jacket and tie. Either a suit or sport jacket with slacks is recommended. Jacket and turtleneck are acceptable. Notice that the most successful handlers are well-dressed with jacket and tie, even in hottest weather. Wash and wear permanent press fabrics which are soil resistant are the best to choose.

Wear well-tailored sport clothes. Don't choose the latest fad or the loudest print. The wrong clothes are apt to draw attention to you and away from your dog. Plain styles and subtle colors or prints are best. Choose a color that contrasts with the color of your dog. Don't wear anything uncomfortable or tight. Keep your jacket buttoned or it will interfere with your handling. Do wear a tie clip. Clothes should be amply cut to allow freedom of movement.

Put your best foot forward in comfortable shoes. Soft rubber soles are noiseless and they give you secure footing on slippery floors. A soft flexible shoe with good support and thick soles is the best for handling.

Don't forget a practical hair cut. Hair falling down in your eyes will distract your every move. Is your dog better trimmed than you are?

For Girls

The winning look for girls has a greater variety. Skirt and blouse, skirt and sweater, suit, jumper, culottes, or dress are all acceptable. Never wear slacks or shorts. The color, style, and material should be attractive on you and be in contrast to your dog. (Example: if you are handling a black Poodle, wear a light colored dress such as yellow or tan to give a good background for your dog.)

Choose a plain tailored look and you cannot go wrong. Some suggestions are: a stitched-down pleated skirt and blazer jacket, an a-line jumper dress (pockets, please) or a sport suit with pleated or a-line skirt. These will be comfortable, fit better, and stay neat-looking longer. You will always look fresh in permanent press fabrics. They are now common in winter and summer weight fashions and many are stain and wrinkle resistant. Save the latest fad for school wear. Don't wear your skirts too short or too long. Remember you must be free to bend, kneel, and run gracefully. Long full skirts or dresses will interfere with your handling and may hide your dog. Don't wear a design or print that will detract from your dog. Don't wear jewelry that will bother your dog or other handlers' dogs. Too many bracelets that jangle are a nuisance.

Check yourself in a mirror at home. Assume the different handling positions and see if your choice of clothes is correct.

Think ahead. Your hairdo should be youthful (10–17), neat, and secure. Your hair should never be in your way while you are handling. Style your hair so that your "lovely locks" cannot fall or blow in your face, or in your line of vision, or become a bother to you in any way.

Make-up for juniors over thirteen should be natural looking. Please keep cosmetics to a minimum and do not use eye make-up.

A shoe-in tie or buckle shoes with soft comfortable soles are the best. No heels, please. Wear either stockings or knee socks. Make sure your stockings are free from runs. Carry a spare pair just in case.

Important—things to have in a emergency:
    Do you have comb or hair brush?
    Clothes brush?
    Spot remover?
    Raincoat you can handle in?
    Needle and thread and safety pin?
    An extra handkerchief?
    Extra shoes or tennis shoes?
    Extra pair of stockings?

Now that you look like a winner from head to foot, go in the ring and be a winner!

When your dog will not
stand for the posing
And he moves 'cross the
ring with a grudge
Just remember the Rule
that is Golden
Keep The Dog Between
You And The Judge

4/ How to Handle
in Junior Showmanship

THIS chapter explains junior competition, the "golden rules of Junior Showmanship" and the ideal Junior Showman. It also includes the treasure of this book . . . six complete handling lessons. To find out how much you have learned, take the test at the end of the chapter.

Junior Showmanship is a competition in which young people are judged on their ability to handle a dog. The prime objective for the junior competitor is to demonstrate his or her ability in showing the dog to its best advantage. Throughout the various ring procedures and examinations, the junior competitor must strive to make his or her dog the most appealing. The points of the dog do not count. The junior must demonstrate that he or she knows the dog's faults and has learned how to minimize them.

Junior competitors must practice the golden rule of JS— **keep the dog between you and the judge.** Whether handling the dog in a show pose or handling the dog in motion, the junior must always keep the dog in full view of the judge.

The ideal Junior Showman must love dogs and enjoy handling them.

The ideal Junior Showman must be business-like in manner and appearance.

The ideal Junior Showman must practice regularly, seek corrective criticism and try to improve all handling skills.

The ideal Junior Showman must study the breed he handles and be knowledgeable of his own dog's conformation.

The ideal Junior Showman must be honest, courteous and considerate.

31

On the Move

STEP 1: How to Walk, How to Run

Toddlers have learned to walk and are just learning how to run. Did you know many juniors have to learn these motions all over again? When you walk to school or run for the bus, your body is in balance and your arms are free. When you handle a dog, your body is slightly turned, your head and neck are turned, and one arm and hand are at work. Therefore, you must adapt to this different position when you handle your dog in motion.

Now, let's begin. Taking the lead in your left hand, extend your left arm at shoulder level. Correct your posture by raising the very top of your head to maximum height.

Look straight ahead and walk across the practice ring. Repeat this exercise taking BIG steps and quickening the pace. Always use a good long stride and adjust your speed to your dog's proper gait.

Use a long stride. Look slightly back over your shoulder to check your dog.

Practice walking several more times and check two problem areas:

(1) Your free arm should be at your side slightly swinging in coordination with your motion. If you have trouble keeping it down either practice swinging it slightly across in front of you by bending your elbow or place your hand in a make believe pocket at your side.

(2)Your head should always remain erect to insure proper posture. When you look at your dog, be sure you turn your head to the side and look slightly back over your shoulder.

Practice the walking exercise until it is correct and natural to you.

Ready to run? All the positions you have just learned in walking are employed in running. The most important feature in this exercise is the size or length of your stride. Take the

longest running step you can, and adjust your speed to your dog's proper gait. Your stride should be strong, straight forward and consistent. Correct and eliminate any bad habits such as running on your toes, leaping in mid-stride or bending your knees more than necessary. You should flex your knees enough for graceful efficient motion. Your knee should never be raised in front of you, nor should it be bent in back of you.

Remember: just because you are running, your posture should not change. If you handle a dog on a loose lead, you must be even more careful to run in an erect position.

STEP 2: Approach to the judge

There are three main reasons for the approach: to keep the dog in full view of the judge when turning to gait, to present your dog courteously for motion evaluation, and to get your dog started in motion before gaiting is examined.

From the right side of the ring, get ready to approach the judge who is in the top center of the ring. See diagram.

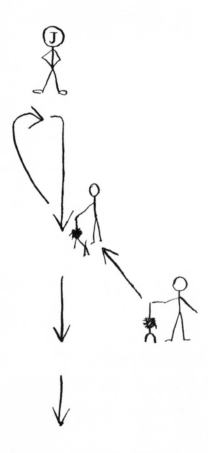

Face in the direction of the judge with your dog at your left side and the lead in your left hand. Walk out to the center of the ring slightly past the judge and turn your dog slowly toward the judge and in a semi-circle in front of the judge. Be sure you keep your handling arm at shoulder height on the turn so that the dog is "heads up" and ready to move.

Now check your position and your dog's position; your backs are to the judge. The lead is still in your left hand. The dog (not you) is directly in front of the judge. The dog is on your left side. Walk across the ring in a straight line. Change hands, turn, and return to the judge. Repeat this exercise without stopping at any point.

The whole idea of the approach is to keep the dog in view and in motion. This exercise should be smooth and effortless. The judge should never have to move to watch your dog gait.

Now try the approach from the left side of the ring. Face toward the judge with your dog on your right and the lead in your right hand. Walk out to ring center. Turn your dog toward the judge and continue in a semi-circle. Leave the judge with the lead still in your right hand and your dog on your right side.

There are two problem areas in this exercise: (1) When you approach the judge and he stops you to give directions, listen carefully and make sure you understand the requested gaiting pattern. Then step aside or, if necessary, turn in a semi-circle so that you are in the proper place to begin the approach. This is difficult and takes practice to look smooth. (2) When you return to the judge and he asks you to gait your dog again, keep your dog in motion by turning in a semi-circle in front of the judge.

Remember: change (the lead) hands on turns *away* from the judge; use a semi-circle turn *in front* of the judge. The only exception to this rule comes when you are handling a very large breed in which case you can turn the dog without changing hands at the end of the ring.

STEP 3: Gaiting patterns.

There are four main gaiting patterns which judges use to examine the moving dog. Junior handlers must be prepared to follow directions and move their dogs in the requested pattern. Let's begin by walking through the **I, L, T,** and **O.**

The "I" Pattern

The "I" is simply down the ring and back in a straight line.

The "L" Pattern

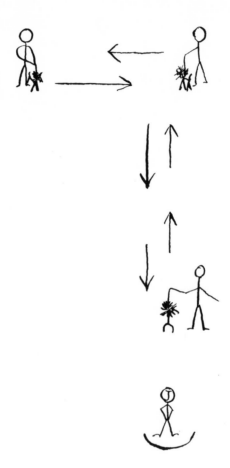

For "L", walk down the ring in a straight line with your dog on your left side. Turn to the left and walk to the corner. Change hands so that the dog is in the judge's view and walk back to the point opposite the judge. Turn without changing hands and return in a straight line to the judge.

The "T" Pattern

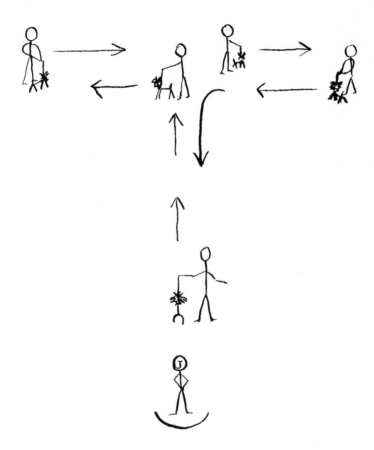

The "T" pattern is very similar to the "L". With the lead in your left hand, walk across the ring. Turn left and walk to the corner. Stop, change hands. Now walk all the way across the end of the ring. Stop, change hands, and return to the point opposite the judge. Return in a straight line to the judge.

The "O" Pattern

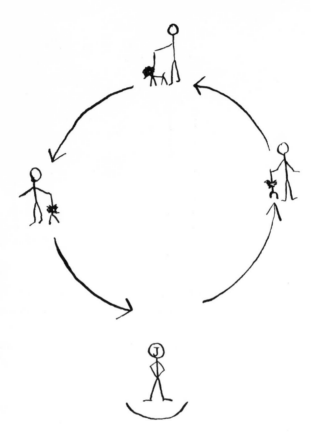

For the "O", hold the leash in your left hand and walk in a complete circle around the ring. This pattern is for individual gaiting and should be done in a circle somewhat smaller than the pattern used for all the dogs gaiting around the ring together.

There is one gaiting exercise which is not a pattern. When two dogs are asked to gait together the handlers are always positioned on the outside of the dogs and the dogs are side by side. Practice this with another person and try to keep the dogs together.

Now that you know what the gaiting patterns are, practice them at your normal speed. Begin with an approach each time.

**Review Steps One, Two and Three
with your dog "on the move."**

Position Is Everything

STEP 4: Setting up your dog.

This lesson starts with homework for you. First you must learn how the breed you handle is correctly posed. Study photographs of ideal specimens and pay particular attention to placement of legs, top line, posture of neck and head, and position of tail. Now observe how the expert handlers pose their dogs to look like the ideal specimens.

Study your own dog. Find out what your dog's good points are and learn how to show them. Know your dog's faults and learn how to disguise them.

Finished your homework? Let's practice. Walk into the practice ring and slowly bring your dog to a stop.

The control of your dog is the basis for every move you make in posing your dog. One hand is always used for control. If you pose your dog without a lead, your control hand will be holding the dog's head or muzzle. If your dog is shown on a lead, your control hand will be holding the short length of the lead.

Your dog is at your left side and the lead is in your left hand. If it applies to your breed, remove the lead slowly and place it near your right foot. As you turn to the side of your dog, change control to your right hand. In the following order, set your dog in the proper pose:

Place the dog's left front foot in position with your left hand.
Change control, to your left hand.
Place the dog's right front foot in position with your right hand.
Change control to your right hand.
Reach under your dog and place the left rear foot.
Place the right rear foot.
Check all four feet (in case your dog has moved.) Kneel on your left knee only. Control remains in your right hand.

Proper setting of front.

Alternate method of setting front.

45

Proper setting of rear.

Proper setting of rear.

46

Correct kneeling position.

Your left hand is used to position the tail. (If this is not appropriate for your breed, your left hand should be at your side.) Make sure your control is skillful. Check the length of lead. It should not be too long or too short. Check the way you hold the muzzle. Your hand should not be in the judge's view.

Remember: this step applies to most breeds but there are exceptions. That is why you must do your homework at the beginning of this lesson. Some breeds are correctly set up by "dropping" them into position. Some breeds are correctly posed by maneuvering the dog into a natural position. Toys are posed with the handler kneeling. Large breeds are posed with the handler in a standing position. In the next chapter you will learn more about the handling of individual breeds.

47

Good balance and maximum reach.

STEP 5: The judge's examination

There are two parts to the judge's examination. First, the judge will examine your dog by touching and feeling major parts of the dog's anatomy. Second, the judge will step back and view your dog as a whole. You must be ready for both types of examination.

Get your dog ready. Let's begin. Walk into the practice ring with the lead in your left hand and bring your dog to a stop at the side of the ring. Pose your dog facing the line of direction and make sure you are in the proper position and posture. Get ready for the judge to approach. (During your practice sessions it is helpful to have someone "play" the part of the judge.) Your right hand is your control hand. When the judge approaches make sure that your hand is not limiting the view of your dog's face and head. When the judge begins to examine

the dog's head, pause to see if you are requested to show the dog's bite. Rise slowly with your back straight and move to the rear of your dog. If you pose your dog on a lead you may need to lengthen it for this position. Keep the lead taut for full control. While you are at the rear of the dog make sure the rear feet and legs are in position and hold the tail appropriately. It is also helpful to place your thumb at the area below and to the side of the dog's tail to prevent the dog from moving back during examination. If you are handling a very small breed it will be necessary for you to be in a squatting position at this time. Do not kneel. Do keep your back straight.

As the judge moves to the left side of your dog to examine the body, be ready to take the dog's head in your right hand and return to the dog's right side. Keep as far away from your dog as your arm length permits so that the judge has plenty of room and a clear view of the dog.

As the judge gets near the dog's hindquarters move slowly to the head and stand directly in front of your dog with both hands used for control. If you pose your dog on a lead, one

At rear of dog, it is helpful to place your thumb at the area below and to the side of the tail, to prevent the dog from moving back during the examination.

As the judge gets near the dog's hindquarters, move slowly to the head and stand directly in front of your dog, with both hands used for control.

hand is proper control. Check the dog's front feet and legs and be ready to move.

As soon as the judge completes the examination return to your dog's right side. Quickly check all four feet and pose your dog. Your posture should be correct here. Your head should be very slightly turned and your eyes should be toward your dog's head. Do not look up at the judge. Now relax your dog and pat him.

Practice this lesson several times. Then practice the examination routine beginning with your dog on the other side.

The most difficult part of this lesson is timing: when to be ready, when to move, when to make your dog look alert. As you practice, think about every move you make. Is it smooth? Is it correct? When you are handling at a show, pay attention to what is going on in the ring. Know where the judge is at all times. Be ready. Be alert.

A small junior with a large dog must use extended arms and legs for smooth handling.

STEP 6: How you and your dog can relax in the ring.

Most Junior Showmanship classes are large and it takes a long time to complete the judging. So you must practice ways to save your energy and your dog's energy and patience. The judge cannot look at you and your dog all the time, so learn to plan when it is possible to relax.

If there are a number of dogs in front of you and the judge has begun his examination, you can relax. But keep your eye on the judge. When the judge is almost ready to examine the dog in front of you, get in position and pose your dog. After the judge is at least two dogs behind you, relax again. While the judge is watching other juniors gait their dogs, you may relax until the dog before you is called out. At that time pose your dog so he looks his best, but have the lead on and be ready to move.

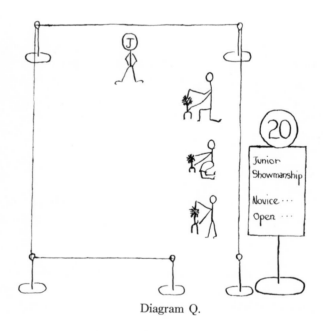

Diagram Q.

The Wide Stride—A Review

Now that you have completed the Six Steps of handling you are ready for the Wide Stride! This is a quiz to find out what skills you must spend more time on. After you have taken your Wide Stride quiz, check the list of tips at the end of this chapter.

Questions:
1. Set your dog in the proper pose. What must you do before you assume the proper position at the dog's side?
2. In Diagram Q (p. 52), you are the third junior in line. Make your approach to the judge. Take your dog straight down and back. Stop. Which side is the dog on? Which hand holds the lead?
3. When two dogs are gaiting together the handlers should be on the _____?
4. How can you check your own posture?
5. In Diagram Q, the judge walks to the last dog in line, walks around to the ring ropes and up on the opposite side of the dogs. Where should the handlers be?

Answers:
1. Check your dog's four feet.
2. Right. Right. (This applies to the handling of all but the very largest breeds.)
3. Outside.
4. Raise the very top of your head as high as possible.
5. Each handler should move to his dog's head, and then to the dog's left side.

Remember: your final test is competing in Junior Showmanship. Study and practice are necessary for all handlers but there is no substitute for actual handling experience.

Important: "relax" in Junior Showmanship is not rest time for you and your dog. For you, it is a time to relax the muscles you use when posing your dog. For your dog, it is a stand-at-ease or occasionally a turn-around in place.

Take your dog into the practice ring and set him in a show pose. Now relax by standing at your dog's head. Pat your dog, and speak to him softly. If the weather is hot and the ring is in the sun, try to stand so that you cast a shadow over the dog's head. In hot weather let your dog relax with mouth open. Practice turning your dog around you. This will give your dog a rest from constant posing. However, be careful not to disturb others near you. Do not let your dog sit or lie down in the ring. You should never sit or talk with others while you are in the ring. Your attention must be on your dog and the judge at all times.

Special Tips

Work slowly, keep calm, don't rush.

Be methodical. Don't fuss and overwork. Don't make unnecessary motions.

Check your own position.

Always keep your back straight.

Use your extended arms to keep a space between you and your dog.

Use your hands in a firm grip but also use your hands to be kind and reassuring to your dog.

Use your legs for raising and lowering yourself so that you can always keep your back straight.

Always know where the judge is.

Be ready for the judge's examination.

Be courteous to others in the ring.

Keep a space between you and the person in front of you. Don't crowd.

Use a squeaker (for certain breeds which should look alert) only when the judge is looking at your dog. It can be very distracting to other dogs.

Leave the dog's brush in the tack box.

5/How to Win in Junior Showmanship

IF it's worth doing, then it's worth doing well. This chapter explains how you can become a Junior Showmanship winner. You will find out how to really look at yourself and how to correct your mistakes. You will learn about the importance of your dog in competition, and how to make sure you have that special knowledge about the breed you handle.

Perfect Your Skills

There must be a reason for every move you make. Your dog's left foot is out of place? Fix it. Know exactly where to place the foot and then leave it alone. You have a reason to make these moves. Can you give a reason for all the moves you make? Are they necessary? Your eagerness and excitement can make you do things which are unnecessary. These moves can be distracting to your dog and can detract from his performance.

Make every move count. Know your dog well and have your dog fully prepared for Junior Showmanship competition.

Every move you make in the ring must benefit the dog you handle. Your moves can make the dog look better, behave better, and feel better. For example: the judge approaches your posed Collie. You know that you must be near the dog's head with proper hand controlling the lead. But how can you make this move really count? Fill this pause at the head with your skill as a handler. Get your Collie "on alert." Present to the judge a view of a devoted Collie watchful and waiting for a command.

Be proud of your accomplishment, be proud of your dog. Jennifer A. Sheldon, Westminster Kennel Club 1965 Junior Showmanship Winner, with her Afghan, Ch. Khabira Shady Lady.

Fortune Favors the Bold

Your attitude toward competing and handling can help make you a winner. It is essential that you enter the ring with a positive outlook. Say to yourself, "I can handle and I want to win." Too many juniors have the mistaken idea that handling to win has something to do with poor sportsmanship. They are defeated before they begin.

Handling to win is the attitude of the experienced and honest competitor. Sportsmanship is how you play the game and how you cope with winning and losing. Remember: you have come a long way as a junior handler and you have learned a great deal. Be proud of your accomplishment. Be proud of your dog. Have confidence in your own ability. Now go in the ring and win!

Apply Polish Where Needed

Your trophies will always be valuable, but they will only look their best when you keep them polished. To be a Junior Showmanship winner, you need polish, too. Polish every handling skill and every motion you make. Pay particular attention to your posture, balance and gracefulness. Discipline yourself to be smooth in handling your posed dog. If you make believe you are in a slow motion film, your handling speed will be correct. Plan your gaiting and turns before the judge calls you out. Remember: the ideal handler uses all necessary skills to put the dog in the spotlight and himself out of notice.

Take a Good Look at Yourself

There are things you do and moves you make that you may not be aware of. Some are handling faults. Some are awkward motions. Some are unconscious gestures.

There are three ways to face your faults:

The best is to have a coach who can watch you at practice sessions and spot your errors. Your coach does not have to be experienced in dogs. It can be someone learning along with you. A parent or friend can follow the handling lessons and tips in this book and find your mistakes for you. Your coach should also watch you when you handle in competition to catch the mistakes you make at a real show.

Professional and amateur handlers who are experienced and knowledgeable in your breed can also be helpful. Ask them for corrective criticisms. Discuss with them the special skills used in handling your breed.

The use of home movies and a large practice mirror will allow you to actually see for yourself. If you have someone film your handling, make sure it includes both practice and competition. A large mirror on the kennel or garage wall will be a great aid when you and your dog must practice alone.

For You and Your Coach

There are a number of mistakes common to most learning handlers. Do they apply to you?

When you are rising from a kneeling position, keep your hands off your dog's back. Don't brace your elbow on your knee while holding your dog's head.

Get rid of the dog brush, while you are in the ring.

To bait is to tempt your dog with morsels. It should never become a display of dog feeding. Also, make sure that it is appropriate to use bait when handling your own breed. If you must bait, keep your actions between you and your dog.

If you use keys or a similar object to alert your dog, do it in a discreet manner. The only reason for baiting or alerting should be the reaction you get from your dog. Again, make sure this procedure is proper in your breed.

Important: the experts you watch do not always demonstrate proper handling. Be sure the skill is correct before you adopt it as your own. Handlers in the breed ring many times change a skill because of the dog they are handling. For example: a particular dog moves better on the right, so the handler keeps the dog on the right in the gaiting patterns.

You must also be sure not to copy a handler's individual mannerisms. There are three common examples of this. When you are kneeling with your dog posed, keep your back straight, head erect and your face turned slightly in the direction of your dog's head. Do not bend your neck or tip your head at some unnatural angle because you see someone else do it. Use a strong, confident, long stride when you run and do not flex your knees any more than necessary. It is unnaturally and physically tiring to bend your whole leg in two. Girls should be confident, athletic and in control—but also lady-like.

Now for personal problem areas. If you wear glasses make sure they are secure and do not slip. Use an athletic band if you wish. Many people who wear glasses have a habit of constantly pushing them back in place or making facial contortions because of the slipping. A handler can't spare his hands for fixing his glasses nor should he be "making faces" to prevent the slipping.

If your hair is distracting in any way, check this problem immediately.

Nervousness and excitement may affect your manners. Don't carry a fixed grin on your face while you're handling, and don't chatter (even to your dog) while the judge is examining it.

Doing What Comes Naturally

Practice and experience equal good handling. You have learned how to handle, how to improve your skills, how to correct your mistakes, and how to eliminate needless gestures. You should be an able handler now. You should be ready to carry out your perfected skills every time you handle. Good handling should be doing what comes naturally.

There is still room for improvement. Your sense of timing in all the things you do will improve with additional experience. You will also gain more poise as you compete. You should be handling well every time you compete. You should have a mature outlook and refrain from making excuses for poor performance.

Is Your Dog An Asset?

"The points of the dog not to count", says the Junior Showmanship rule. But now that you are an accomplished handler and are ready for top Junior Showmanship competition, you must take a good look at your partner. The best dog for Junior Showmanship does not have to be a great example of its breed. However, there are some important requirements.

Your dog must be a specimen of at least average quality. Intelligence, patience and good spirit are necessary. Your dog must be intelligent enough to respond to training, patient enough to endure the long Junior Showmanship classes and have sufficient spirit to move willingly at all times.

Your dog can help you win. If your dog is eye-catching, attention will be drawn to you. If your dog responds well to your handling, you will appear skillful and capable.

Your dog may also limit your success. An unruly or impatient dog will not provide the handler with the opportunity to demonstrate handling skills. A sluggish dog will only draw unfavorable attention to the handler. If the dog does not behave or respond properly to the handler, its action shows that little preparation has been made at home.

One of our personal anecdotes may help you understand the value of a good Junior Showmanship dog. Rellim was a big good-natured Setter. He was not the finest example of his breed but he was very attractive, carried a lovely coat, and had a fun-loving manner. Bethny trained him and practiced with him daily. He knew exactly what she expected of him and never let her down. However, Junior Showmanship judges became critical and said that the big Setter was so easy to handle that Bethny had very little to do to show him. Bethny solved that problem by tickling Rellim occasionally to make him move a foot. And, of course, she continued to win under the critical judges.

Remember: it's a team that competes in Junior Showmanship. You and your dog must know each other, like each other and work well together. The noted professional handler, Art Baines, once told us, "Show that dog 'til the ribbons are given out. Don't ever give up."

That Special Knowledge

To achieve excellence in handling you must know the background of the breed you handle so that you can present the dog in characteristic form and mood. It is a mistake to get between the judge and your dog. It is just as big an error to handle a Terrier in the same way as a Sporting Dog. Each breed is presented in a different way. For example: there is a difference in spirit and structure between the English Setter and the Irish Setter. Therefore, there are handling differences in these two breeds.

Are you ready to specialize your handling skills? You will find special handling tips on certain individual breeds at the end of this chapter. These tips also apply to similar breeds. Before you begin, make sure your dog is trimmed and groomed appropriately for its breed. Find out what type of show lead is proper and select one carefully.

SPORTING

The breeds in the Sporting Group were developed and used for hunting game. They are capable, attractive and devoted hunting companions. While the degree of discipline in training may vary, all of these dogs are properly handled in a gentle manner. The classic pose of a Sporting Dog should give the impression of a confident, well-mannered dog, willing and able to please its master.

All of the Sporting breeds are posed without lead. The handler kneels on one knee and holds the head and tail.

There are specific ways of holding the tails of various breeds. For example, the Pointer tail must be sloping downward from the body, but is supported across the fingers with the hand flat.

English Setter: The English Setter head is held so that it is on a line parallel to the ground. The nose should not be pointing up or down. The topline is level or slightly sloping from the withers to the root of the tail. The front feet are placed so that the legs are parallel when viewed from the front. When

62

viewed from the side, the front legs are well under the dog and are straight. The rear feet are placed apart and back enough to give the dog a correct top line. When viewed from the side, the hocks must be straight up and down (perpendicular to the ground). From the rear view, the hocks must be parallel.

When standing at the head of the English Setter, the handler places the dog's ears flat along the sides of the head and muzzle and holds them there. This gives a clear view of the neck. The tail must be held so that it slopes slightly downward from the root to the end. Four fingers or the first two fingers grasp the end of the tail on the judge's side and the thumb is on the handler's side.

Don't ever make it look difficult to handle the Setter. This breed is known as a "Gentleman By Nature". Keys, bait and squeakers are out of order here. They only detract from the relaxed dignity of the dog. Use bait only if absolutely necessary when gaiting. Do it discreetly.

A word about Cocker Spaniels. Remember, these are Sporting Dogs. Let them do their own walking in the ring. Don't carry a dog that should be an able hunter.

HOUND

The breeds in the Hound Group were also developed to hunt. The scent Hounds and sight Hounds have very different jobs and so they differ greatly in appearance. From the dignified, aloof Afghan to the intelligent, audacious Dachshund, there is great variety and individuality among the Hounds.

Pat Leary LeMoigne advises, "The Afghan handler must try to match the grace and timing of the breed in motion. It takes great patience to coax the best from this breed. They cannot be forced. Use a light hand to guide them. Develop a sense of timing and rhythm in both moving and posing your dog. I used to hum to myself for improved timing."

Whippet: This classic sight Hound possesses many individual characteristics. The Whippet must be handled in a gentle manner. The handler should seek to give the impression that this dog is alert, capable and distinctive. Pose the Whippet with the lead on. Adjust the length of lead so that your control hand does not detract from the view of the dog. Be precise with your hand movements so it does not appear that you are over-handling.

Present the head properly. Use your free hand to point the dog's muzzle straight ahead. This must be a subtle guiding motion only. Keep your dog's attention so that the ears will be in the characteristic alert.

Place the front feet so that the legs are straight and parallel when viewed from the front, and beneath the dog when viewed from the side. Place the rear feet so that the topline is well arched over the loin, the stifles well bent and the hocks perpendicular to the ground. The tail can be guided into the proper tucked position by the handler, but is not usually held.

Susan Gilman says, "To really show a dog you must be able to speak through your hands. If your dog has a fine topline, slowly sweep your hand along the dog's back. But be very casual and never obvious. A Whippet can be more difficult to handle than it appears. You must know how to get your dog happy in the ring."

WORKING

Man has used dogs to help him with many tasks. The breeds which have been developed to carry out these tasks are proud, courageous, alert and strong. The appearance of the Working Dog is always impressive. All breeds are on lead when posed.

Collie: The handling of this unusually beautiful breed involves almost all technique and very little motion. The Collie standard includes two statements concerning the presentation of the breed. "The Collie shall stand naturally straight and firm," is in the general description. The standard then specifically states, "When the Collie is not in motion, the legs and feet are judged by allowing the dog to come to a natural stop in a standing position so that both the forelegs and the hind legs are placed well apart, with feet extending straight forward. Excessive 'posing' is undesirable."

The Collie handler must prepare his dog well to be able to present it properly in a natural position. The lead is used to guide the dog to stop in a proper pose. With the use of a fine choke chain collar and a nylon snap lead you can set the dog up just by applying pressure on the lead. If hand positioning of the rear feet is necessary it must be done in a subtle manner. The Collie handler must hold the lead so that the dog stands with neck slightly arched and upright. When posing the dog,

Ann Bowley says, "The Collie is a wonderful breed to work with—a pleasure to show and a joy to watch if the handler and dog make a graceful team."

the handler stands at the side and holds the lead in the hand which is closest to the dog's rear. This leaves the hand nearest the dog's head free for keeping the dog alert.

The handler must present the dog in proper pose and at alert without distracting activity. Techniques used to alert the dog and set the ears erect are timed just before the judge's examination.

When showing the Collie the handler stands in front of the dog, and with as little activity as possible keeps the dog in pose and at alert.

Characteristic expression is very important and the able handler must use skill and perfect timing to have the dog look appealing at the necessary moment. The key to much of the success in handling this breed is to start show training early. Make it fun and establish a spirit of friendship with our dog.

Use bait or keys or toys but only when their use is necessary. Continued use of these items when the judge is not nearby is annoying to others.

Please, when you are standing in front of your dog appealing for his response, don't constantly use your knee to check his advance. This is unappealing and takes away from the overall impression you should be trying to achieve.

TERRIER

Fearless, incredibly active and clever are characteristics which mark the dogs bred to pursue vermin and small game. The Terriers more than any other group have a common personality trait. They possess boldness, determination and appear "full of fire". All the Terriers are posed on a lead and the handlers kneel during the pose (except for the Airedale).

Scottish Terrier: The dapper Scotsman must be a picture of ready courage. The task of the handler is to accentuate Terrier characteristics and the individual dog's good points. This breed, like most Terriers, is properly "dropped" into the pose. The lead is raised to lift the front feet off the floor and then lowered just enough to set the front. The rear is dropped by lifting the dog, with hand placed between the hind legs and allowing the rear legs to fall into position naturally. This technique is less time consuming and when done properly, produces excellent results.

It is not incorrect to set the foot by hand. However, a Terrier should be "handled" as little as possible. It should always appear that the dog is independent of the handler. Make sure the lead keeps the dog's neck in an upright and slightly forward position. The muzzle assumes a natural position with nose on a lower plane than the eye. It is imperative that the handler present a very alert, prick-eared dog. The front legs are straight, or very slightly bent, with clean sloping lines from shoulder to foot when viewed from the front. The rear legs have well-bent stifles and the area from hock to heel is straight. The tail is posed high in a very slight curve toward the back. It is proper to use the flat of the four fingers to support the back of the tail. The only part of the hand in the judge's view is the fingertips. Sparring or encouraging the dog to demonstrate Terrier spunk toward other dogs should be limited to the breed ring.

Edward Van Istendal says: "Accentuating topline, length of tail, furnishings, general appearance and disposition are the continuous moves that a good handler makes. Sparring is only appropriate when done with another Terrier that is supposed to spar."

Barbara Worcester Keenan (West Highland White Terriers) advises: "When deciding whether to set or drop a Terrier, determine which has the best results for your dog. The rear of the lighter-weight Terriers may be dropped by lifting from the butt of the tail. This is not appropriate for the heavier breeds."

Deborah Duguid (Airedale) says, "When you handle the king of the Terriers make the dog look and feel like a king. When the judge comes to look at your dog, or when your dog has just finished gaiting, throw something on the ground to attract the dog. This will produce that alert expression and prick ears. At the end of gaiting it also helps bring the dog to an even stop. Win or lose, reward your dog in some way at the end of the class."

TOY

The Toy breeds have existed for centuries and have remained popular as devoted companions. Once principally the delight of royalty and those of great wealth, the breeds in the Toy Group are varied in appearance. From the saucy little Chihuahua to the dramatic, beautiful Pekingese, to the slender, elegant Italian Greyhound, these dogs possess courage and intelligence. Because of their very small stature and the fact that they are properly posed on a table, Toys are difficult for use in JS.

The lead is not removed from the Toy when in pose. It is permissible for handlers to kneel on both knees when handling these breeds. However, keep the balls of your feet on the ground and do not kneel with your shins on the floor. Never move around your dog while in a kneeling position.

The Do's And Don'ts of Handling a Maltese:

Daryl Martin demonstrates the special etiquette in handling a Maltese. Her Lhasa Apso models in several of the photos but the skills shown are appropriate to both breeds.

1. Correct handling of Toys on a table. Don't be on top of your dog. No unnecessary touching of dog. Keep proper distance. Hold leash properly. Keep brush out of view.

2. Improper handling on the table. Lead all over the dog. Overhandling of face and tail. Handler leaning directly on top of the dog obstructing judge's view.

3. Technique peculiar to Toy handling. Headstudy: call attention to a good head by holding the head gently so the judge can see it.

4. The improper way of showing the head. Handler is holding the head in an unnatural position. The dog's face is distorted. The fingers have lifted and disturbed the hair.

5. Proper gaiting. Lead not too short or too long. Keep your dog with you and alert to your wishes.

6. Improper gaiting. The dog is too far behind the handler. Lead is too long. Dog not properly gaited for the size and temperament.

7. Proper baiting technique. Hold bait slightly in front of dog but keep your body behind the dog to provide a contrasting background for the light dog. Hold the leash tightly on top of the dog to keep the neck high.

8. Improper baiting. This is a clumsy, unbalanced position. The handler detracts from the dog's stance.

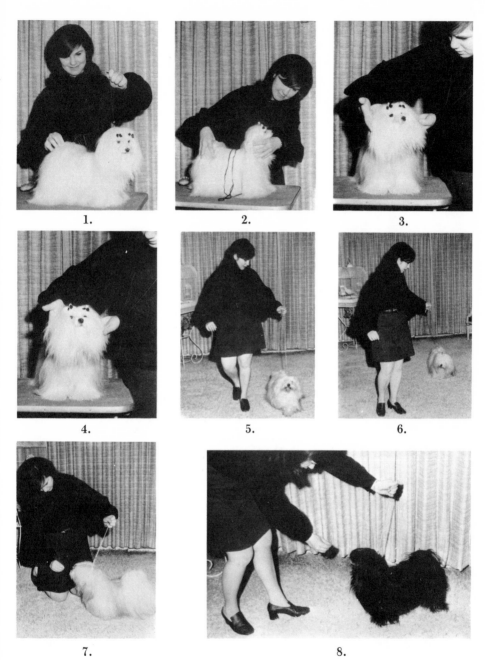

1.

2.

3.

4.

5.

6.

7.

8.

NON - SPORTING

Most of the breeds in the Non-Sporting Group are unrelated. Their origins were linked to specific tasks, such as guarding, hunting or fighting. The appearance and temperament of the various breeds are as different as their origins. Contrast the Poodle's great beauty and air of distinction with the massive and courageous Bulldog. The breeds in the Non-Sporting Group are posed with leads on and, except for the larger dogs, the handler is in a kneeling position at the side of the dog.

Bulldog: The task of the Bulldog handler is to create the overall impression of a massive, courageous yet peaceful dog.

Present the head with attention to details peculiar to the breed. The lead is placed on the neck so that the two loose pendulous folds between jaw and chest are prominent. The hand holding the lead should be out of the immediate area of the dog's head. The free hand may be used to guide the head to a face forward position or to check the lay of the flews or the chops.

The front feet of the Bulldog are positioned so that the legs are straight from the elbow to the foot, when viewed from the front. From the side, the legs fall in a straight line between withers and feet. Elbows are well out away from the body. The rear feet are positioned so that the rear legs form an

Cody Sickle and his Bulldog, Cherokee Morgan.

almost straight line from hip bones to feet when viewed from the side. The hock is only slightly bent. From the rear, the feet are wide apart to allow sufficient width between the turned out stifles. Bulldog handlers must note that it is characteristic to have hocks turned slightly toward each other and rear feet turned outward.

6/Let's Play
Twenty Questions

THE questions in this chapter are some of those most often asked by juniors. These questions have been taken from the letters we have received over the past ten years.

1. **How can I find a pen pal who is interested in dogs?**

    The major magazines which have JS columns compile a list of pen pals regularly. Send your name, address, age and breed interest to the columnist.

    Did you know that Lydia Coleman Hutchinson and Marsha Hall Brown were pen pals before they met in the JS ring?

2. **Why are dogs "handled?"**

    Dogs are "presented," "handled" or "shown" so that the judge can examine and observe each entry thoroughly and without delay. The handler is providing a service and showing courtesy by making the judge's examination as easy as possible.

3. **Just what is Junior Showmanship?**

    Junior Showmanship Competition is the class at a dog show at which the handling merits of junior contestants are judged.

4. **Who can judge JS?**

    Any professional handler or any judge licensed by the American Kennel Club, may be invited to judge the Junior Showmanship classes.

5. **Why don't all shows have JS?**

    It is the decision of the show-giving clubs to include JS classes. Unfortunately some clubs do not realize the importance of JS.

6. What other countries have JS?

Canada and Australia.

7. How can we start a junior kennel club?

How to form the club:

Go to your nearest kennel club (breed or all-breed) and ask them to approve a junior division. (All junior clubs should be affiliated with an adult organization.)

The kennel club should appoint an adult chairman and/or committee to help and advise the junior group.

All interested juniors should be invited to join. Hold a "planning" meeting. The junior club should elect officers with the assistance of adult advisors. Junior officers and adult advisors should study the by-laws of the parent club and work out suitable by-laws for their junior division.

Set a membership fee. Make it reasonable in amount.

Juniors should plan and carry out their own club activities. The adult chairman and/or committee should serve in an advisory capacity.

8. Our breed club would like to encourage juniors. What is the best way we can do this?

There are three steps to a good beginning:

1. Provide Junior Showmanship information to the young people in the club and if possible organize a class of instruction for them.

2. Offer an annual award for the best Junior Showman in the club.

3. Include junior news in club newsletters, bulletins or magazines.

9. Can a female in season be handled in Junior Showmanship?

Yes. However, we strongly recommend that tablets and sprays be used for the dog to minimize the problem. Only an experienced and completely responsible junior should be expected to compete under these conditions. If there is any evidence that the dog's presence in the ring is disruptive or presents a danger to the safety of other dogs or juniors, the junior handling the bitch in season should leave the ring.

10. Our Junior Kennel Club is compiling a library for members' use. Can you suggest some helpful books for juniors?

Dog Care for Boys and Girls, by Blanche Saunders
Dog Training for Boys and Girls, by Blanche Saunders

International Encyclopedia of Dogs, Howell Book House
White House Pets, by Margaret Truman

There are many helpful booklets. *The AKC Rules and Regulations* and Popular Dogs' *"Your First Litter"* and *"Your Puppy at Home"* are examples. Your local library can suggest books of dog fiction.

11. I have been entering JS at point shows. Am I still eligible for Junior Showmanship at match shows?

Yes. However, after you have placed consistently at point shows it would be a courtesy for you to limit your match handling to the breed ring.

12. I am in charge of trophies for an all-breed club. Please suggest prizes for Junior Showmanship.

We humbly suggest that this Handbook would make a very appropriate prize. Pen and pencil sets, scrapbooks and photo albums are popular with juniors. Dog items such as leads, tie clasps and pins are also appreciated but a gift certificate at a "show shop" is even better. The most thoughtful thing a club can do is to reward every junior who does not win or place with a token of some kind. Candy, ball point pens, pads and even gift-wrapped Milkbones have been given at shows.

13. Is there any age limit for juniors handling in regular breed classes?

No. However, it is important that the junior be experienced enough to have full control over his or her dog. Also it is only common courtesy to the judge that the junior be competent enough to handle the dog and to follow directions.

14. I am going to several shows in Canada. Will I be able to compete in Junior Showmanship?

Yes. Junior Showmanship is very similar to competition here.

15. What do you have to do to become a handler?

There are two ways in which a person may apply to become a "professional". First, at the age of 18, you may apply to the American Kennel Club for permission to apprentice under a licensed and approved professional handler. After successfully serving the apprenticeship, and upon reaching the age of 21, you may apply for a handler's license.

16. What is the Exhibitors' Educational Trust?

Begun in 1962 in honor of the late George F. Foley's 80th birthday, and originally named for him, it is a junior scholarship fund for deserving dog fanciers. Recently renamed the Exhibitors' Educational Trust, it awards grants annually to young men and women who plan careers in veterinary medicine. Applicants are judged on scholastic ability, participation in the dog fancy, character and financial need. The fund operates entirely on contributions from organizations and individuals in the sport of dogs. For applications or donations, write The Exhibitors Educational Trust, 125 High Street, Boston, Mass.

17. My dog is purebred and can be entered at shows but he is not show quality. It is the only dog I have for Junior Showmanship. What can I do?

Under the present Junior Showmanship rules a dog can be entered for "JS Only" as long as it is eligible for shows. However, it would be to your advantage to have another dog to handle. Many breeders and exhibitors are very interested in helping juniors and are sometimes willing to give deserving juniors co-ownership in a dog. Talk to other members of your breed club or write to its secretary or junior chairman. Many times, juniors earn the privilege of co-ownership by helping in the kennels, exercising dogs and assisting the owner at shows.

A Junior Showmanship dog, our Bo'Sun, was handled to title by both of us. He was also handled in Junior Showmanship over the years by Charles Capace, Betty Lou Ham, Sally Sly, Laurel Howe and Elizabeth and Bethny Brown. At the age of 12 he is still helping young people learn how to handle.

18. Why don't juniors stop competing in Junior Showmanship after they have compiled their qualifying wins for Westminster?

Junior Showmanship is a success because it is an open competition based on initiative and personal achievement. A junior may compete as little or as often as he wishes. He may exhibit any breed he owns. Most important, he has the right to accumulate as many wins as he or she is able. If a junior cannot qualify for Westminster, he or she has not earned the honor of being there. Dogs in competition are not limited only to a share of wins and then retired to allow other dogs to score. Annual awards are based on consistent achievement throughout the year. Juniors must compete often and win often to receive such awards.

19. How can I get a job working in a show kennel for the summer?

Write to kennels in your area stating your age, experience and interest in dogs. An advertisement in a large all-breed or breed club newsletter might be helpful. Professional handlers often need extra help in the summer months. Write to handlers near you, or discuss your work interest with handlers at shows when they are not busy. You might also consider work in an animal hospital or grooming shop. Read your local newspaper for help wanted listings.

20. Are certain breeds easier to win with in Junior Showmanship than other breeds?

A highly skilled junior will win in Junior Showmanship regardless of the breed of dog being handled. It is true, however, that there are certain breeds (Setters, Pointers, Afghans, Doberman Pinschers, Boxers, to name a few) that are eye-catching. These breeds provide a good opportunity for the junior to demonstrate handling skill. The breeds most difficult for use in Junior Showmanship are the very large and the very small. It is a difficult job to cope with a Newfoundland and look relaxed as well as competent. It is even more difficult to "shine" with a Toy breed. Rarely are juniors judged on table handling etiquette which is the major skill in showing a Toy.

It is interesting. to note that juniors have won with just about every breed. Some juniors have turned a seemingly difficult breed into their chief asset by becoming so skillful that the dog looks remarkable. The best example of this is the great success of Cody Sickle and his Bulldogs. He made those Bulldogs outclass the merriest Setter and the most dignified Dobe.

7/Particularly for Parents

TO be the parent of a Junior Showmanship competitor is physically, emotionally and financially taxing. You have, no doubt, often wondered whether you will survive the next competition.

While your junior is at a school pep rally, you are making out the entries and checks for the next show. A special scout meeting is called for the night the dogs are to be bathed and the car packed. And your junior, so exhausted from the merry whirl of activity during the week, sleeps for the three hours it takes you to drive to the show. Then, while your junior becomes completely involved in handling (with varying degrees of skill) in Junior Showmanship you can only stand nervously at ringside and try not to talk to yourself or weep in public.

To be the parent of a Junior Showmanship competitor is also a treasured experience and a great pride. To help your own child practice and master the skill of handling a dog you are both fond of, is the beginning of a mutual interest. The travel, the grooming, exercising, and waiting are never time measured in hours or minutes but in "time together". The first time your junior does a good job of handling, or gets a placing, or finally wins the pink ribbon, there is much to share. And when your junior qualifies for Westminster, or wins an annual award, or finishes a champion, you will find that your time and work and moments of disappointment are overshadowed completely by the pride and joy in your junior's accomplishment.

Words to the Wise

Before great plans are made for junior competition, a parent must determine whether the junior wants to handle and whether the junior is ready for competition.

Father and son combination at the shows: William P. Gilbert ("Mr. Great Dane") and William J. Gilbert.

A junior should enter Junior Showmanship only if:

He or she can control the dog at all times.
He or she has some knowledge of ring procedure and can follow the directions of the judge.
The junior is emotionally mature enough to understand and accept winning or losing.
The junior likes dogs and is thoughtful of his dog's well-being.
The junior wishes to participate.

Wise parents will help the junior at practice sessions at home and encourage handling at match shows first. When the junior enters competition the parent must assume the role of guide and advisor only. If there is a question for the judge or ring steward before or after the competition, the junior should seek the answer.

Thoughtful parents will praise the junior immediately following competition for all the good points demonstrated and refrain from any criticism until the next practice session at home. To teach the junior the ideals of sportsmanship the parent must practice good sportsmanship. The wise parent should try to limit the discussion of competition to the positive aspects involved. Pointing out other juniors who are competent or who perform a particular skill well, and discussing the judges who are helpful and thorough, make constructive conversation.

When a particular competition is difficult and not successful for the junior, a helpful parent can guide the junior's thoughts to the next show and the next chance in the ring.

Parents should encourage their juniors to congratulate the winner of Junior Showmanship classes. Juniors should also receive some instruction from parents concerning appropriate manners when they win.

The practical parent will help the junior learn about care, health and training of dogs. Daily responsibilities for juniors are recommended. Simple chores should be the task of beginning juniors, and older or more experienced juniors should be capable of more difficult duties.

The understanding parent will know that it is necessary for a junior to enjoy activities in other fields. The parent should encourage participation in sports and hobbies, membership in youth groups, and time spent at social activities at school or in the community.

Sense and Sensibility

Of course the parent provides the junior with the dog, financial support, transportation and a cheering section of at least one. But the responsibility of a parent is not that simple.

There are rules governing Junior Showmanship. Every junior must know these rules and follow them. The parent must see to it that his or her junior is honoring all rules.

The parent is responsible for the appearance and demeanor of the junior. Planning and preparation at home will help the junior realize the importance of appropriate attire and the necessity of good manners.

The safety of all juniors in competition is the responsibility of the parents of those juniors. The parent must be certain that the junior he or she sends into Junior Showmanship has the knowledge and physical ability to control the dog at all times, especially in crowded conditions. The dog must be considered. A parent must choose a dog of stable temperament and be sure it is suitable for a young person to handle. The parent should

81

Dog shows make for togetherness.

also instruct the junior in the thoughtful treatment of the dog both in and out of the show ring.

Help Wanted

Parents can help juniors and Junior Showmanship most by:

Helping the all-breed clubs provide for Junior Showmanship at shows.

Offering trophies or prizes for Junior Showmanship classes; submitting a list of knowledgeable and available judges for Junior Showmanship classes.

Encouraging a breed club to offer annual junior awards for juniors handling that breed in Junior Showmanship and regular classes.

Offering obedience and field awards.

Offering time or financial support to insure the continued success of the club's annual junior award.

Extending a helping hand to parents and juniors just beginning.

Being good sports themselves.

Keeping a sense of humor.

8/ You Can Be
A Six-Star Junior

★
★
★
★
★
★

FOR Junior kennel Clubs as well as for juniors everywhere this is a program of learning. This basic outline can be simplified, shortened, modified or added to so as to meet the needs of the group's interests and age range. It is intended to help juniors become more aware of a great variety of dog-related activities. It is also aimed at preparing juniors to be of service in a variety of ways to "Man's Best Friend."

MEET . . . GO . . . SAVE . . . HELP . . . DIG . . . DO . . . are the six units of activity. To complete a unit, choose five of the suggested activities and carry them out. When a junior completes all six units, he or she shall be a Six-Star Junior.

MEET!

This activity unit is to help make club meetings different and interesting and to encourage all members to participate.

Complete five of the following (numbers 1 and 5 are required):

1. Be in charge of planning for at least one meeting.
2. Present part of the program at a meeting.
3. Teach a skill.
4. Know how to introduce a speaker, welcome a guest or new member.
5. Give a book report or read a short article from a magazine or newspaper on a dog-related topic.
6. Be in charge of ordering a film to show at a meeting.
7. Make up a simple game or quiz for members to play.
8. Demonstrate a simple handling or training technique.
9. Plan a panel discussion.
10. Plan and help prepare a debate.

GO!

This activity unit includes suggested field trips. Choose five from the following (number 3 is required):

1. Visit a dog officer or dog warden.
2. Visit a Humane Society, dog shelter or pound.
3. Visit a veterinary hospital.
4. Visit an established kennel.
5. Visit or take part in a dog training class.
6. Visit the working place of a professional in the field of dogs. Example: handler, groomer, photographer, artist, etc.
7. Attend a show, trial or other organized dog event.
8. Visit a pet shop.
9. Take snapshots of one of your trips and make a scrapbook.
10. Go to a museum or art gallery and discover dogs as presented by artists.

SAVE!

This activity unit is most important for all juniors. Dog health, safety and first aid knowledge is necessary for all dog fanciers. The help of a veterinarian is suggested for some of these activities. Choose five of the following (numbers 1, 3 and 6 are required):

1. Know how to groom and trim your dog properly. Know why it is essential to care for nails, teeth, ears and coat.
2. Learn the proper diet for your dog and know how much exercise your dog's needs daily.
3. Find out what diseases your dog is susceptible to and learn how to prevent them. Know what internal and external parasites might affect your dog's health. Learn how to control these problems.
4. Show that you can take a dog's temperature and administer medicine in liquid or tablet form.
5. Discuss the proper way to bathe a dog. Bathe your own dog. Know how to use powder and liquid preparations for removal of fleas, ticks or lice.
6. Be able to give first aid for the following: wounds, internal injuries, electric shock, fractures, hemorrhage, burns, shock, drowning, suffocation and animal bites.
7. Know the first aid and proper medical treatment for a person who has been bitten by a dog.

84

8. Make an emergency muzzle and show how to use it. Know the use of a dog lasso and restraining stick.
9. Know how to approach an injured dog and what safety precautions are necessary for you and the dog.
10. Know the care of a brood bitch and learn how to care for a newborn litter.
11. Learn the laws in your community and state concerning dog ownership, dog control and unclaimed dogs. Know how to contact the nearest animal shelter.
12. Find out the humane and professional method for destroying animals.

HELP

This activity unit is to introduce juniors to the many fields of dog services and to help juniors be of service. Choose five of the following (number 5 is required):

1. Find out how stray and/or injured animals are cared for in your area. If possible, visit the nearest shelter. Learn the local and state laws which pertain to unclaimed dogs.
2. Find out how and why dogs are licensed in your area. What are the fees and how are they collected and used?
3. Learn how guide dogs are selected and trained for the blind.
4. Learn how dogs are used in one of the following categories: police work, military service, search, guarding (schools and buildings.)
5. Participate in one of the following suggested activities, or with your group select a project or activity which would be of service to your area. Give at least 20 hours of your time to this project.
   a. Organize, help to organize or work at a town rabies clinic.
   b. Help your town or city with dog licensing by helping to take a dog census, or do simple office work.
   c. With your parent club or members of the parent club plan and carry out a dog demonstration at a school, hospital or children's home.
   d. Volunteer to help your local Humane Society.
   e. With your parent club or members of the parent club plan and carry out a public demonstration for Dog Week or Be Kind to Animals Week.
   f. Find out what services the following groups provide: Orthopedic Foundation for Animals, Humane Society of the United States, American Society for the Prevention of Cruelty to Animals, The Seeing Eye.

DIG

This activity unit is to help juniors understand and appreciate the dog today by digging into the past.

Choose five of the following (numbers 1 and 8 are required):

1. Study the basic structure of the dog. Learn the parts of the dog by name. Study the skeletal formation of the dog and know the names of the major bones.
2. Read about the earliest history of the dog and find out what animal group it belongs to.
3. Find out how purebred dogs originated. Learn the origin of your favorite breed and how it has developed to the present day.
4. Learn how man has used dogs for specific purposes in the past. Know at least four main uses of the dog today.
5. Read about famous dogs in history.
6. Read at least one book about a dog.
7. Know three authors noted for their dog stories. Read about one of these authors.
8. Learn the AKC standard for your favorite breed. Explain it at a club meeting.
9. Become familiar with three famous works of art featuring the dog. Know the artists' names and when the paintings or sculptures were done.

DO

This unit is to help juniors learn more about and participate in organized dog activities. Choose five of the following (number one is required):

1. Participate in one of the major fields of the dog activity (show, obedience or field.) Learn to handle and become familiar with the rules of the competition.
2. Learn how to make out an entry form and how to make a catalog.
3. With members of your club or with the parent club plan and carry out a match show, fun field trial, or handling competition.
4. Select a field of activity (other than the one you specialize in) and learn more about it. Attend a show or trial.
5. Find out about other regular dog activities such as herding, drill teams, hound packs, racing, dog sled racing, and tracking and search. Find out about the handling and training of some of these.
6. Know how a dog earns title in your selected field or activity.
7. Compare shows or trials in the United States with those held in another country.
8. Find out the regulations pertaining to the shipping of dogs by air.

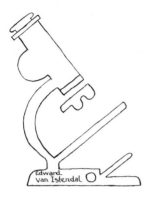

Edward
van Istendal

9/ Looking Ahead . . .
Careers for You

HAVE you thought of how dogs will fill your future? Have you ever considered filling your future with dogs? Your interest and experience as a junior fancier can be a valuable first step toward a career of life-long avocation. The following opportunities in dog-related fields include professional and semi-professional careers, full time and part-time occupations, and leisure time involvement.

Veterinary Medicine
There are many and varying career opportunities for a Doctor of Veterinary Medicine. Aside from private practice, either individually or in groups, the DVM may choose research, teaching, public health work, meat inspection, disease control, or conservation and ecology. Veterinarians are employed by universities, hospitals and laboratories. They work for the federal, state and local governments, with the Peace Corps and the military. Drug companies and dog food companies need qualified doctors on their staffs.

87

If you are considering veterinary medicine as a profession, these are suggested preparations:

College preparatory course in high school with emphasis on science and mathematics.

Participation in school and club activities, sports or hobbies.

Some kind of experience with sick and injured animals — take a part time job with a veterinarian if possible.

Scholastic average of B or higher. Girls will find that requirements demand much higher grades of them.

Check with veterinary schools for their college course requirements so that you can plan to take the necessary subjects.

It takes between six and eight years to become a veterinarian. Four years of veterinary school is preceded by two, three and sometimes four years of college training.

This career demands high scholastic ability, hard work, determination and dedication to science and animals. It is interesting and exciting work with personal and financial rewards.

Animal Science

A new program in the field of animal science has created interesting new careers and has filled a great need in veterinary medicine. The educational program now being offered at universities in New York, New Jersey, California, Maine and Maryland consists of a two-year college course in animal science for the training of semi-professional veterinary assistants and technicians.

Career possibilities include work in medical centers research institutions, government health agencies and animal hospitals and clinics. Graduates would work under veterinary supervision and would be trained to take over all mechanical, secretarial and routine maintenance duties. They would also prepare animals for surgery, prepare and dispense certain medications, apply first aid and apply and replace wound dressings.

Applicant requirements:

High school graduates with a sincere interest and regard for animals.

Graduate of an approved high school or passing the State University Admissions Examination.

Previous credits in mathematics and science including chemistry.

Animal Science graduates are in great demand and salaries are commensurate.

Dog Photographer

The dog photographer must be highly skilled in his or her profession, must enjoy dogs and people, must possess endless patience, and must be willing to travel. Dog photographers must also have a basic knowledge of breed characteristics and proper show poses.

There are official photographers at all dog shows. These professionals are listed in the show catalog by the show giving club. They perform two basic services. They record on film the winners of the show from Best of Breed to Best in Show.

They also are available at the dog owner's request to record other wins or activities of the day.

This area of dog photography is difficult work. Long hours must be spent traveling and working away from home on weekends. Clear photos must be produced regardless of weather, lighting or show sites. Developing and mailing keep the photographer working long hours between shows. Often dog owners and magazines request rush orders for photos of show wins in order to meet publication deadlines.

Dog photographers work in a variety of other places. Many schedule private appointments for special pictures and portraits during the week. A photographer may be hired by a large kennel to record on film the various dogs in residence. Several noted dog photographers specialize in taking unusual candids of children and dogs. Photographers are in demand to cover

Bill Gilbert, Junior Showman, Assistant Handler, Licensed Handler, Official Dog Show Photographer. Bill began his photographic career with training he received in the United States Navy.

such dog related events as obedience, field and retriever trials, herding events and tracking and search tests.

Many dog photographers work in advertising. From dog food to grooming supplies to medical preparations, photographs of dogs are used to sell most products.

A career in photography can be interesting and financially rewarding. Professional training, practical experience and knowledge of dogs are all necessary prerequisites. After high school graduation the future photographer should seek enrollment in a technical school, college or night school which offers a complete program in photography. Experience in simple photography can be gained by taking pictures for school clubs, newspapers, socials and sports events. Taking photos at dog training classes, handling classes and match shows can be a learning experience. The study and observations of animals and dogs is important. The future dog photographer should attend shows and other dog events and visit kennels.

Dog Training

The variety of careers and employment opportunities for the dog trainer is almost endless. Man uses the dog in so many ways and in so many places that capable dog trainers are always in great demand.

Obedience training for dogs has become very popular not only as a basic service to the pet owner but to the obedience trial enthusiast. Training classes and obedience schools are sponsored by towns and organizations all over the country. Instructors at these schools teach owners how to train their dogs. There are also professional trainers who own or work for private dog training schools. These dog trainers work primarily with dogs sent for training.

Dogs are used for hunting, racing and herding and must be trained accordingly. Training kennels are maintained where dogs may be sent for field trial training, retriever trial training and for breaking gun dogs and hunting hounds. Racing dogs also require special training. Herding dogs are a great aid to livestock owners, and large ranches many times employ a trainer and handler for the dogs.

There are dog trainers in the entertainment field. Any time dogs appear in plays, movies, and on television, it represents long hours of work on the part of a skilled trainer.

Valerie Fisher, of Seattle, Washington, the youngest handler in history to train and handle a dog to Field Trial championship, gives a command to her famous AFTC Misty's Sungold Lad, CDX. This amazing young trainer has taken the most coveted national awards for field work. She is also an accomplished obedience trainer.

The greatest service the dog provides for man is as a guide for the blind. The most highly skilled trainers are necessary for work in programs like The Seeing Eye. They must work with the dogs, the future owners and the staff specialists.

Guard and sentry dogs are trained for use in the military, for police work and for private use. Most of the professional dog trainers in this category have received their career training and experience while serving in the armed forces. Those trainers who leave the military often are employed by state or local police.

Dogs must be trained for patrol duty, search and criminal apprehension. In recent years dogs have been trained and used as reliable narcotics "agents." They have been used at customs stations, post offices and shipping ports.

Tracking dogs are also trained and used by police. Bloodhounds have led police to many suspects and have found many injured or lost people. Trainers are needed to supply the growing demand for guard dogs in schools and industries.

There are so many different and specialized careers in dog training that it is impossible to include information on instruction and preparation. However, it is advisable to learn basic training procedures by gaining experience in obedience work. It would also be helpful to seek summer employment or part-time employment at a kennel or school where dogs are trained for some type of work. Many young people, particularly 4-H Club members, volunteer to provide foster homes for future guide dogs.

Dog Artist

"Stop, Look, and Listen" is the advice to the junior who aspires to be a dog artist. Before you take pen and ink or brush and canvas in hand, stop and take the time to observe all forms of animal life. Watch both wild and tamed animals in their natural settings and while in motion. Observe the difference between the old and the young, the male and the female. Look at dogs of all breeds. Educate your eye by training, trimming and caring for dogs. Study breed characteristics and coat textures. Then listen to some practical advice.

Patricia Detmold, well-known for her water colors of animals and wild life, specializes in dog portraits. Pat won her first Children's Handling class at her first competition in Montreal, Quebec, Canada in 1946. She has successfully bred, trained and handled Sporting dogs for show, field and obedience.

A career as an artist, especially when it is limited to animals and wildlife, might be a financial risk in the beginning. The future dog artist should take basic art courses in high school and plan further study at a college, technical school or art school which offers a well-rounded program. Commercial art and art education graduates will find interesting employment opportunities and be able to work in the field of dog art in spare time.

To be successful, the dog artist must have some background in biology, anatomy, animal and dog history, breed characteristics, and technical art skills. Remember: the artist must be able to produce quality work and satisfying likenesses. The artist also must be able to portray hunting dogs afield and working dogs on the job.

Professional Dog Handler

A licensed professional dog handler grooms, conditions, trains and shows dogs for other people and is paid for his or her services. The successful handler is a specialist in the field of dogs, a good businessman and a tireless traveler. Since almost all dog shows are scheduled on weekends, the handler spends almost the entire week on the job. It is a difficult and demanding career. But the variety provided by the dogs, clients, travel and contemporaries makes it most interesting.

Qualifications — Professional Handler applicants must be twenty-one years of age. The American Kennel Club screens applicants carefully and requires that the future handler be knowledgeable, experienced, responsible and financially stable. The applicant must submit records of show experience and achievement and produce proof of adequate kennel facilities.

Preparation — Since there is no school or training program, it is the task of the individual to prepare for this work. It is essential to be experienced in the sport of dogs and to attain a high degree of skill as a trainer, handler, conditioner and groomer. This knowledge can be acquired through employment with an established breeding kennel or a professional handler's kennel. A fundamental knowledge of running a business, keeping records and handling correspondence is necessary. The future handler must also know about canine health, maintenance and first aid. Driving experience, including city and freeway situations and a valid driver's license, are musts. AKC rules and regulations and the handler's code of ethics must be studied.

Application for a handling license may be requested from the AKC. Names of applicants are published in the *Pure-Bred Dogs — The American Kennel Gazette* and are then considered by the AKC for approval or disapproval.

Juniors should keep accurate show records now. You may need these later for a handler or judge's application.

Apprentice Handler

Future handlers may train for their profession by working as an apprentice handler under the supervision of an AKC-approved licensed handler. Young dog fanciers of 18 to 21 years of age interested in this method of preparation must

Charlotte Stacy, former Junior and now a professional handler, judges Patty Proctor and Kathy Del Deo in Junior Showmanship.

apply to the AKC for a license. They must successfully complete the apprenticeship and be at least 21 years of age before applying for a regular handler's license.

Dog Care

There are many career and business opportunities in the field of dog care. Boarding and grooming establishments employ many people. Humane Societies and dog pounds must be staffed by skilled workers. Veterinarians and animal hospitals need non-professional help. The newest business in this area of work is the dog walker.

The owner and operator of a boarding kennel must have the proper facilities for keeping dogs and must know the state and town ordinances for kenneling dogs. He or she must be responsible, experienced in the care of dogs, and capable of keeping dogs healthy and the facilities clean and in good repair.

Kennel workers must like dogs and demonstrate responsibility in caring for them. Duties will include feeding, providing water and cleaning kennel areas.

A professional dog groomer must be skilled not only in proper trimming and bathing methods but must have knowledge of breed standards and basic canine anatomy. To be successful a groomer must also know how to cope with unruly animals and those not accustomed to electric clippers, nail clippers and tools used to clean teeth and ears. A future groomer must learn how to care for the variety of tools and equipment used and how to keep them clean.

Several states now have excellent schools of dog grooming. The New York School of Dog Grooming was the first and is licensed by the State Department of Education. It offers three courses: instruction for pet owners, the basic course for professional groomers and the advanced course. The duration of the professional course is one month. The curriculum also includes instruction for future grooming shop owners and managers.

Many of the job opportunities in dog care provide on-the-job training. Young people can gain valuable experience by working at kennels, animal hospitals or grooming shops during summer vacations or on a part-time basis.

It is important that applicants for these jobs have high school diplomas or the equivalent and have good character references. For those who plan to be self employed and especially for those who will be employing others, a basic course in business is recommended.

Dog Show Judge

There are approximately 2,500 men and women who are licensed by the AKC to judge at dog shows. These authorities perform the task of evaluating the conformation and gait of the dog. The judge must examine each dog and determine how it "measures up" to the written standard for its breed. Then the judge must decide which dog comes closest to the standard description.

Some judges are approved by the AKC to judge only one or two different breeds. There are judges who may judge all the breeds in one of the six groups. There are also judges, called all-rounders, who judge all recognized breeds.

The great majority of judges donate their time and services or request a fee which will simply cover expenses to and from

96

Former Junior and now one of America's youngest judges, Lydia Coleman Hutchinson.

the show. In most cases, only those judges who are qualified to judge many breeds and are long experienced receive fees of a professional nature.

The role of a judge requires long experience, study and knowledge of all phases of the dog fancy. The judging of dogs is fascinating and rewarding. However, long hours in the ring under all kinds of weather conditions make this job physically and mentally tiring.

Application for a judge's license may be requested from the AKC. Any person over the age of twenty-one who is in good standing with the AKC and has had experience in purebred dogs may apply. The applicant must be prepared to list personal statistics, give a reason for wishing to judge and submit records of breeding and showing. He or she must also write about the breed or breeds applied for and answer questions about the AKC rules and regulations.

If the name of the applicant is authorized for publication it will appear in the next issue of *Pure-bred Dogs — The American Kennel Gazette.* Two months after the original publication the AKC Board of Directors will act upon the application and if it is approved, the name of the applicant will be listed as "provisional judge." After the completion of three judging assignments the applicant must wait for the board to make a final review. If it is a favorable action the applicant becomes a judge.

Pure-Bred Dog Breeder

The fundamental role in the sport of dogs is that of the breeder. It is the most difficult role and many times the most discouraging. It can also be the most rewarding. The future of purebred dogs is in the hands of those who spend their leisure time as breeders.

There are no formal qualifications, but the following will serve as a guide to those interested in this field.

A conscientious breeder must have one basic goal — to improve the quality of his chosen breed. Those who would breed dogs for the fun of it, or as an experiment, are selfish. Those who think only in terms of producing litters to sell are cruel (humane societies report regularly on the critical problems of canine overpopulation.) Those who continue haphazard trial and error methods are a detriment to the breed.

The breeding of dogs is not a self supporting hobby. The financial responsibility must be met and understood. The price of a quality brood bitch is high. Stud fees, veterinary services, kennel facilities, equipment and food are essentials. Personal responsibilities include daily care of the dogs and maintainance of the kennel facility.

Preparation for becoming a breeder should include a secure knowledge of the breed standard, and an understanding of pedigrees. The concepts of linebreeding, inbreeding and outcrossing, and the study of dog anatomy, heredity and reproduction are necessary. The future breeder should also have a working knowledge of canine health, nutrition and first aid.

Unfortunately, there is no formal training provided for the breeder. Each will have to seek knowledge and gain experience through his own efforts. Read books, newsletters and magazines. Attend dog club meetings, seminars, clinics and lectures. Visit kennels, animal hospitals, training classes and dog shows. Investigate the curriculum at the nearest college or university for courses which might help you.

10/Junior "Hall of Fame"

THIS chapter is a salute to the winners of Junior Showmanship over the years. The juniors pictured here represent the finest competitors and handlers in the United States and Canada. You will see juniors from all over the country handling a great variety of breeds of dogs. Some are Westminster Junior Showmanship winners, some are High-Score Junior Showmanship winners, and several are noted for their achievement in breed handling. You will learn that many of these juniors are still active in the dog world. They are breeders, handlers, judges, kennel owners and managers and some are even the parents of today's junior showmen.

The photographs we have chosen to use in this chapter have been selected to show the junior champions from many different breeds and parts of the country. We know that there are many noteworthy juniors not included. We also regret that there were some juniors whom we were unable to reach.

99

Betsy Long Burr
Long Island, N.Y.
Collies.
First place winner at Westminster's Children's Handling class, 1941. Sorry, no photo available.

Dorothy Long Hale
Long Island, N.Y.
Collies.
Junior Handling winner at Westbury Kennel Club, 1936. Best Obedience Handler at Westchester KC while still a junior, 1939.

Dorothy Long
Betsy Long

William P. Gilbert
Flemington, N.J.
Great Danes.
Competitor in Children's Handling, Westminster, 1942; Assistant Handler's license, 1946; Professional Handler's license, 1955. From leash to lens—now an official dog show photographer. Bill is pictured handling to Best in Show at Lancaster KC, 1964.

Patricia Detmold
Glen Garner, N.J.
English and Gordon Setters,
Brittany Spaniels, English Cocker
Spaniels.
Children's Handling wins included: Berwick, Nova Scotia,
1944; Halifax, Nova Scotia, 1945;
Montreal, Quebec, 1946. Patricia
bred and trained many champions, as well as dogs for Field and
Obedience. Now a dog artist.

Barbara Worcester Keenan
Montclair, N.J.
West Highland White Terriers, Fox Terriers, and Scottish Terriers.
Barbara is pictured with her first Westie,
who later became Ch. Edgerstoune Cindy,
foundation bitch of Wishing Well Kennels,
home of 40 champions with wins of 50
Bests in Show. Top win, Best in Show with
Westie, Ch. Elfinbrook Simon, at Westminster KC, 1962.

101

Lydia Coleman Hutchinson
Westport, Conn.
Cairn Terriers and Toy Poodles.
Lydia is pictured at age 11 with the first dog she made a champion, Cairn Terrier Ch. Shagbark Misty Betts. Lydia scored 15 Junior Showmanship wins between 1949 and 1954. They included: Second at Westminster KC Junior Showmanship; First at First Company Governor's Footguard Athletic Assn.; First at Eastern DC, Boston. Her Ch. Bonnie Bairn of Wolfpit was top Cairn bitch in the U.S. for 1955–57, and her Miniature Poodle, Ch. Hollycourt Merry Spirit was Winners Bitch at Westminster in 1955. She gained a judge's license in 1964, and is licensed for all but six of the Terrier breeds, for the Terrier Group, and for all varieties of Poodles.

102

Marsha Hall Brown,
Greenville, R.I.
English Setters, Irish Setters,
Gordon Setters, Beagles, Bassets and Collies.
Marsha, co-author of this book,
is pictured at first Junior Showmanship win at Willimantic,
Conn. 1950. Her Junior Showmanship Firsts included: Providence County KC, Eastern Dog
Club at Boston; First Company
Governor's Footguard Athletic
Assn. at Hartford; Framingham
KC. Winner of the Gaines
Youth Award, 1955. Marsha
has bred and handled English
Setters to championships, has
been a licensed handler, vice-president of the English Setter
Assn. for five years, and is the
Junior activities columnist
for *Popular Dogs.*

Left:
Betty Kemp Crossman
Greenville, R.I.
English and Gordon Setters.
Junior Showmanship wins include: First at
Montpelier, Vt.; First at Champlain Valley
KC; First at Providence County KC; and
First at First Company Governor's Footguard Athletic Assn. at Hartford. Betty
finished two Gordon Setters to championships.

George Alston,
Pasadena, Md.
Winner of Westminster Junior Showmanship, 1954. Now a licensed handler,
George and his wife, Mary Ann, own
Fieldstone Kennels, offering facilities
for boarding, grooming and training.
Specializing in Poodles and Sporting
dogs.

Patricia Leary LeMoigne
Pottersville, N.J.
Afghan Hound.
Pictured winning Westminster Kennel Club Junior Showmanship in 1956. Best of Breed at Afghan Hound Club of America Specialty at New York.

Ray Sumida
Monterey, Calif.
Irish Setters and English Setters. Ray, the California Junior Handler of the Year in 1954, is an experienced handler of over 20 breeds. Pictured scoring Junior Championship win at Oakland, he was also Best Junior Showman at Golden Gate, 1956. Member, California Professional Handlers Assn.

104

Patricia Matson Alston
Long Island, N.Y.
English Springer Spaniels
Junior Showmanship winner at Westminster
KC, 1957.

Robert Harris
Long Island, N.Y.
Boxers, Beagles.
Second at Westminster KC Junior
Showmanship, 1957. Stewards
Club of America, Top Boy Handler 1956–1957.

Bethny Hall Mason
Greenville, R.I.
English, Irish, and Gordon Setters, Afghans, Pointers, Beagles and Schipperkes.
Winner of Westminster KC Junior Showmanship, 1959; third at Westminster, 1956, '57; Best Junior Showman at First Company Governor's Footguard Athletic Assn. at Hartford, 1958; First at Eastern Dog Club, Boston, 1955, '56; Stewards Club of America, Top Girl Handler 1956, '57, and '58. Gaines Youth Award, 1959. Junior columnist for *Popular Dogs.*

Right:

Charlotte Martin Stacy
Virginia Beach, Va.
Cocker Spaniels.
Junior Showmanship wins included First at Eastern Dog Club, Boston, and third at Westminster, 1958. Charlotte is pictured handling Ch. Bo-Art's Back Talk to Best in Show at Lewiston-Auburn KC, 1959. She is now a licensed professional handler, together with her husband, W. Terry Stacy, specializing in Cocker Spaniels. Also an Obedience trainer.

Nancy Kelly
Conn.
Golden Retrievers.
First in Westminster Kennel Club
Junior Showmanship, 1958.

Jean Owen Parkhurst
Southington, Conn.
English Setters, Pointers, Dachs-
hunds.
Pictured in win of Best Junior
Showman at First Company
Governor's Footguard Athletic
Assn. at Hartford, Conn., 1960.
Also Junior Showmanship winner
at Elm City KC at New Haven,
and at Great Barrington, Mass.
Junior showmanship finalist at
Westminster in 1959, '60 and
'61. Jean trained and handled
several English Setters to their
championships.

Jennifer Sheldon
Massapequa, N.Y.
Afghan Hounds.
First in Junior Showman-
ship at Westminster in
1965, after having been
Second in 1962, '63 and
'64. Pictured handling to
all-breed Best in Show at
Scranton, Pa., she also went
BIS with her Afghan at
Devon, Pa. Handled Afghan
to Best of Opposite Sex win
at Westminster, two years,
and Rottweiler to Best in
Specialty at Trenton.

Anna Maria Stimmler Burke
Fairview Village, Pa.
Maltese and Poodles.
Obedience award winner, 1958.
Winner of High Score Trophy
for most Junior Showmanship
wins in 1962 (awarded in 1963).
Best Junior Showman at First
Company Governor's Footguard
Athletic Assn. at Hartford, 1963.
Third in JS at Westminster, 1963.
Handled Maltese, Ch. Co-Ca-He's
Aennchen Toy Dancer to First in
Toy Group at Westminster, 1964.
Scored 8 Bests in Show and 24
Firsts in Toy Group with her
Maltese.

Clare Hodge
Bryn Mawr, Pa.
Whippets.
Winner of Junior Showmanship at
Westminster, 1964.

William Coleman
Durham, N.C.
Beagles.
Breeder of four litters of Beagles.
Winner of five Firsts in Junior Show-
manship, including pictured win at
Vineland, N.J., 1964.

Ann Bowley
Woodruff Collies
Durham, N.H.
Collies, Briards.
Best Junior Handler, Collie
Club of N.H. 1965; National
4-H Dog Care and Training
Champion award winner,
1964; Junior Handling 4-H
State Champion, 1963 and
1965. Handled Collies to wins
of Winners Bitch and Best of
Opposite Sex at Westminster,
1966, '67, '68 and '70. Winners
Bitch with Briard, 1969.

Left:
Richard Van Istendal
Hatboro, Pa.
Keeshonden and Scottish Terriers.
First winner of Novice and Open at Valley Forge KC
Junior Showmanship. Finalist in Westminster JS, 1966.

Right:
Edward Van Istendal
Hatboro, Pa.
Keeshonden and Scottish Terriers.
Recipient of the George F. Foley Educational Trust Award,
1970–71 (Penn State University). Finalist in Westminster
KC Junior Showmanship, 1964, '65 and '66.

Above:
Deborah Duguid
Toronto, Ont., Canada
Airedale Terriers.
Best Junior Handler at Syracuse, N.Y.
Won three consecutive JS championships
at Ottawa, 1965, '66 and '67 to gain
permanent possession of Doris Courtney
Trophy. (Pictured in 1966 win.) JS winner
at Chagrin Valley KC, Ohio, for two years,
and a finalist at Detroit for two years.

At left:
Melody Stoltz
Sun Valley, Calif.
Toy Poodles, Boston Terriers, Italian Grey-
hounds, Yorkshire Terriers, Lhasa Apsos,
Shih Tzus, and Welsh Terriers.
Best Western Junior Handler, 1969. First
in JS at Beverly Hills KC, 1968. Finalist
in Westminster KC Junior Showmanship,
1969.

Linda Young
West Newbury, Mass.
Irish Setters, Boxers, Harriers, Dachshunds, and Cockers.
Junior Showmanship wins include: First at South Shore KC, 1956; First at
Springfield KC, 1967; First at Champlain Valley KC, 1966, '67; and Second
at Westminster KC, 1967. Handled Winners Dog Irish at Combined Setter
Specialty in New York, 1968.

David Lynn Brumbaugh
Perry, Georgia
Pomeranians, Labrador Retrievers, Miniature Schnauzers.
Pictured scoring First in Junior Showmanship at Westminster KC,
1967. David owns and breeds Miniature Schnauzers.

Laurel Howe
Westfield, N.J.
English Setters.
Junior of the Year, Hudson English Setter Club, 1965–1969. Winner of the English Setter Association of America Junior Showman Award for 1965, '66, '67 and '68, and runner-up in 1969. Winner of 24 Junior High Score awards.

Cody Sickle
Evanston, Ill.
Bulldog
Finalist in Westminster KC Junior Showmanship. Pictured wiinning Best in Show with Ch. Cherokee Morgan at Mid-Hudson KC in 1969.

Above:
Daryl Martin
Highland Park, Ill.
Lhasa Apsos, Maltese and Shih
Tzus.
Pictured handling Maltese to
Best Brace in Toy Group at
Westminster 1969 under judge
Anna Katherine Nicholas. Twice
winner of First in Toy Group at
International KC at Chicago.
Daryl has won 15 Bests in Show
and 25 Group Firsts with her
Maltese, Ch. Martin's Jingles Puff
and Ch. Martin's Bangles Puff.

At right:
Susan Gilman
Nashua, N.H.
Whippets.
First win at Maryland KC, 1964.
Winner of High Score Trophy
for 1965 and 1967. Second, West-
minster Kennel Club Junior
Showmanship, 1970.

Top:
Kimberly Haigler
Fullerton, California
Irish Setters, English Springer Spaniels, Australian Terriers.
Winner of 13 Firsts in Junior Showmanship. Winner, Irish Setter Club of America Annual Junior Award, 1968 and 1969. Pictured with Ch. Michael's Patty O'Shea, Best of Breed and Group third at Sacramento, Calif.

At right:
Melissa Beth Brumbaugh
Perry, Georgia
Miniature Schnauzers, Maltese, Pomeranians and Labrador Retrievers.
Junior Showmanship wins include Miami, Fort Worth, and Memphis. Pictured winning Toy Group with Maltese at Macon, Ga. 1970 under judge Haskell Schuffman.

116

Heidi Shellenbarger
Costa Mesa, California
Whippets, German Shorthaired
Pointers, English Cocker Spaniels
and Cairn Terriers.
Junior Showmanship Firsts at
Ventura Dog Fanciers, 1970;
Beverly Hills KC, 1970; and
Westminster KC, 1971. Heidi put
major points on Ch. Gretchenhof
Newporter with Winners Dog
win at Sir Frances Drake KC,
and was Best of Opposite Sex
with the Whippet, Ch. Gretchen-
hof Sea Witch at Orange Empire
KC.

Charles A. Westfield III
Huntington, N.Y.
Bulldogs and Chows
Junior Showmanship wins include First
at Eastern Dog Club, 1968, and Thirds
at Westminster KC, 1970 and 1971. Has
handled Bulldog to wins of Bulldog Club
of Connecticut Specialty 1970, and breed
and Group third at Mid-Hudson KC. Handled Chow in win of Best of Breed (3-pt.
major) from puppy class at Burlington
County KC, 1968.

11/Junior Crowns

JUNIORS wear many crowns. In this section you will find a list of these special awards and titles and a short description of the competitions.

International Junior Showmanship Champion

The JS Competition held at Westminster Kennel Club show at New York's Madison Square Garden is the only international junior competition. Juniors who qualify in Canada are eligible to compete along with juniors from the United States for the famous Leonard Brumby Sr. Memorial Trophy.

For many years this competition consisted of one class of winning juniors, judged by one licensed professional handler. The first place winner of this class was named the top junior handler of the year.

However, now this competition is held in two sections. Two different judges preside over these classes. A third judge presides over the competition of the finalists and names a winner, a second, a third, and a fourth.

There has also been a change in the number of first place JS wins needed for eligibility. Juniors must now have won five or more competitions in an Open Division of Junior Showmanship at dog shows held under American Kennel Club rules where championship points were awarded. These five wins must have been made when the juniors were no younger than 10 years of age and no older than 16. The shows must have been held during the period between the Westminster Kennel Club shows.

Top Southern Junior Handler

In 1970 the first regional competition was held for juniors in the Southern states. Juniors who reside in the following states are eligible to qualify: Alabama, Arkansas Florida, Georgia, Louisiana, Mississippi, North Carolina, Oklahoma, South Carolina, Tennessee and Texas. One first place in the Open JS class at a participating kennel club show qualifies for this annual competition. The competition is held each year at different Southern shows and consists of two preliminary classes and a final competition.

Top Rocky Mountain Junior Handler

The first annual competition for juniors who reside in the
following states will be held in 1972: Arizona, Colorado, Idaho,
Kansas, Montana, Nebraska, New Mexico North Dakota, South
Dakota, Utah and Wyoming. One win in the Open JS class at
a participating kennel club show qualifies a junior for the
competition to be held at shows in the eleven state area.

Kennel Club of Beverly Hills Junior Championship
Los Angeles, California.

The Harry Sangster Memorial Trophy is awarded to the winner
of the annual junior championship competition held in conjunc-
tion with the Beverly Hills Kennel Club's summer show. Juniors
must have won at least one Open JS class during the year to
qualify for this annual competition.

First Company Governor's Footguard Athletic Association
Hartford, Conn.

The Governor of the State of Connecticut offers the trophy to
the junior judged Best Junior Showman at the Hartford show
JS competition each year. The winners of the JS classes at this
show compete for the Governor's Trophy.

International Kennel Club
Chicago, Ill.

The JS competition at Chicago is one of the largest in the
country. This coveted win is the goal of many top junior showmen.

Ottawa Championship Show, Ottawa, Ontario, Canada

The Doris Courtney Trophy is awarded to the top winning
junior showman in the JS classes each year. A junior must win
this award three times to gain permanent possession of the
trophy.

The Annual High Score Award

Each year the Annual High Score Trophy is presented by *Dog
World* to the junior who wins the most number of JS firsts
during the year.

119

Ray Sumida, California Junior of the Year, 1954.

Christine Pulscher, Houston, Texas. Winner of the first Top Southern Junior Handler Award 1969. Chris handled her Basenji to the top spot at Shreveport, La., 1970.

To
Marsha Hall
Girl Show Dog Fancier
1955

In recognition of exceptional participation and achievement in organized dog activities as determined by a board of judges in a competition sponsored by the

Gaines Dog Research Center

New York City, March 12, 1956.

Anna Maria Stimmler Burke, Fairview Village, Pa., receiving trophy from Governor John Dempsey for Best Junior Handler at Hartford, Conn. 1963.

Annual Breed Club Awards

Many breed clubs offer awards to junior members for achievement in JS. Information concerning these awards should be requested from the club secretary or awards chairman. (The English Setter Association of America was one of the first to sponsor annual junior awards and at present offers trophies for JS, breed handling, Obedience and Field.)

The following three awards, listed for the record, are no longer offered:

*Champion Junior Handler of California, Oakland, Calif.

To compete for this annual title and trophy a junior had to win at least one JS class during the year and be a resident of California. The competition was held after the JS classes at the Oakland Show.

*The Stewards Club of America Award

This trophy and the title "Top Winning Junior Handler of the Year" was presented to the junior boy and junior girl who scored the greatest number of JS wins during the year.

*The Gaines Youth Award

Four youth awards were presented annually by Gaines Dog Research. A boy and a girl "Show Dog Fancier of the Year" were selected as well as a boy and a girl "Field Dog Fancier of the Year." Nominees (sponsored by dog clubs and organizations) were judged on service, participation and achievement in the field of dogs.

121

Westminster Kennel Club Junior Winners

1933 First Children's Handling winner not recorded.
1934 Winner not recorded.
1935 Winner not recorded.
1936 Dorothea McAnulty
1937 Winner not recorded.
1938 Arthur Mulvihill, N.Y.
1939 Mona Saphir—Old English Sheepdog.
1940 Jerry Werber, N.Y.
1941 Betsy Long, N.Y.—Collie.
1942 Betty Hinks
1943 Walter Wilson—Gordon Setter.
1944 Betty Bolger, Pa.
1945 Evelyn Straubmueller
1946 Frank Hill, Pa.
1947 John Herr, Lancaster, Pa.
1948 George Metz, N.Y.—Boston Terrier.
1949 Monica Rumpf, N.Y.
1950 Hope Johnson, West Hartford, Conn.
1951 Theodore Hallender, Mass.
1952 William Henry
1953 Phyllis Campbell, Rhode Island—Great Dane.
1954 George Alston, Pa.—Boxer.
1955 Mary Donnelly, N.J.—Irish Terrier.
1956 Patricia Leary, N.J.—Afghan.
1957 Patricia Matson, N.Y.—Springer Spaniel.
1958 Nancy Kelly, Conn.—Golden Retriever.
1959 Bethny Hall, R.I.—Irish Setter.
1960 Allen Kirk, Va.—Scottish Terrier.
1961 Betty Lou Ham, Mass.—Irish Setter.
1962 Susan Heckmann, Maryland—Dachshund.
1963 Lydia Ceccarine, N.Y.—Boxer.
1964 Clare Hodge, Pa.—Whippet.
1965 Jennifer Sheldon, N.Y.—Afghan.
1966 Laura Swyler, N.Y.—Wire-haired Dachshund.
1967 David Lynn Brumbaugh, Ga.—Miniature Schnauzer.
1968 Cheryl Baker, Mass.—Pointer.
1969 Charles Garvin, Ohio—Dalmatian.
1970 Patricia Hardy, Ohio—Golden Retriever.
1971 Heidi Shellenbarger, Calif.—Whippet.

American Kennel Club
Regulations for Junior Showmanship
(Effective September 1, 1971)

Note: These regulations implement the following dog show rule:

A Club or Association holding a show may offer Junior Showmanship if it so chooses. The classes and procedure shall conform to the American Kennel Club regulations governing Junior Showmanship, as adopted by the Board of Directors.

Section 1. **Approval of Classes.** Any club that is approved to hold a licensed or member all-breed show or a specialty show held apart from an all-breed show, may also be approved to offer Junior Showmanship competition at its show.

Section 2. **Standard for Judging.** Junior Showmanship shall be judged solely on the ability and skill of the Juniors in handling their dogs as in the breed ring. The show qualities of the dogs shall not be considered. Junior handlers shall not be required to exchange dogs. The judge must excuse a handler and dog from the ring if, in his opinion, the handler cannot properly control the dog.

Section 3. **Approval of Judges.** Any person who is eligible to be approved to judge one or more breeds at AKC licensed or member shows, and any licensed handler, may be approved to judge Junior Showmanship, but no person approved to judge Junior Showmanship at a show shall handle any dogs at that show; nor shall any dog owned wholly or in part by the Junior Showmanship judge or by any member of his immediate family or household, be eligible to be entered at that show. However, a member of a licensed handler's family, if he or she also holds a handler's license, may handle dogs owned by others at the show where the handler is judging Junior Showmanship. The name and assignment of each judge shall be included in the list of judges sent to AKC for approval. Junior Showmanship entries shall be included in computing judges' assignments under Chapter 10, Section 13 of the Dog Show Rules. A judge will not be disapproved for a Junior Showmanship assignment because of its proximity in time and distance to another Junior Showmanship assignment. Any change in judges shall be handled in accordance with the Dog Show Rules.

123

Section 4. **Classes and Divisions.** The regular Junior Showmanship classes shall be:

(A) *Novice.* This class shall be for boys and girls who are at least 10 years old and under 17 years old on the day of the show and who, at the time entries close, have not won a first place in a Novice class at a licensed or member show.

(B) *Open.* This class shall be for boys and girls who are at least 10 years old and under 17 years old on the day of the show, and who have won a first place in a Novice Junior Showmanship class at a licensed or member show. The winner of a Novice class shall automatically become eligible to enter and to compete in the Open class at the same show.

(C) *Junior and Senior Classes.* Either or both of these regular classes may be divided by age into Junior and Senior classes, provided the division specified in the premium list. A Junior class shall be for boys and girls who are at least 10 years old and under 13 years old on the day of the show. A Senior class shall be for boys and girls who are at least 13 years old and under 17 years old on the day of the show.

(D) *Classes for Boys and Girls.* Any or all of these regular classes may also be divided by sex to provide a class or classes for Boys and a class or classes for Girls, provided the division is specified in the premium list.

(E) *Best Junior Handler.* A club offering Junior Showmanship may offer a prize for Best Junior Handler provided the prize is offered in the premium list. The Junior handler placed first in each of the regular Junior Showmanship classes, if undefeated in any other Junior Showmanship class at that show, shall automatically be eligible to compete for this prize.

Section 5. **Armbands.** Armbands with the catalog numbers of the dogs shall be worn by the Junior handlers.

Section 6. **Eligibility of Dog.** Each dog handled in a regular Junior Showmanship class must be entered and shown in one of the breed or obedience classes at the show, or must be entered for Junior Showmanship only. Each dog must be owned or co-owned by the Junior handler or by the Junior handler's father, mother, brother, sister, uncle, aunt, grandfather or grandmother, including the corresponding step and half relations. Every dog entered for Junior Showmanship must be eligible to compete in Dog Shows or in Obedience trials. At a Specialty show, each dog must be of the breed for which the show is held.

A dog that has been excused or disqualified by a breed judge or by a Bench

Show Committee may still be handled in Junior Showmanship if eligible to compete in Obedience trials. A dog that has been rejected, dismissed or excused by the veterinarian for the protection of the other dogs at the show or for the protection of the dog excused, may not be handled in Junior Showmanship.

Section 7. **Premium List.** A club that has been approved to offer Junior Showmanship must list the classification in its premium list, with a description of the entry requirements for each class offered, and the name of the judge of each class. The number of entries in any or all classes may be limited, provided the limits are specified in the premium list.

Section 8. **Entry Forms.** To be acceptable each entry form must meet all of the requirements of Chapter 16, Section 4 of the Dog Show Rules, and in addition must be checked in the space provided to show that the dog is to be shown in Junior Showmanship, and must show in the spaces provided on the back of the form, the Junior Showmanship class in which the Junior handler is entered, the full name, address, and date of birth of the Junior handler and, if the dog is not owned or co-owned by the Junior handler, his relationship to the owner. The identification slip for the entry of the dog shall show the entry in Junior Showmanship and the class.

If a dog is to be handled in more than one Junior Showmanship class by different handlers of the same family, a separate entry form must be submitted for each Junior Showmanship class and each Junior handler.

Section 9. **Closing of Entries.** Entries for regular Junior Showmanship classes shall close at the same time that entries close for the show.

Section 10. **Judging Program.** The judging program shall list the Junior Showmanship classes, the ring(s) in which they are to be judged, the name(s) of the judge(s), the hour of judging, and the number of entries in each class.

Section 11. **Catalog.** The information on any dog entered for Junior Showmanship only shall be listed at the end of the listing of its breed or variety. The dog's catalog number, the breed, and the name of the Junior handler shall be listed by classes under a separate section for Junior Showmanship.

Section 12. **Ribbons and Prizes.** The color of ribbons or rosettes for Junior Showmanship classes shall be:
First Prize—Rose
Second Prize—Brown
Third Prize—Light Green
Fourth Prize—Gray

125

They shall be at least 2 inches wide and approximately 8 inches long, and shall bear a facsimile of the AKC seal, the words Junior Showmanship, the name of the show-giving club, and the date.

No money prizes shall be offered. All other prizes must be described or value stated, and must be offered for outright award. No prize may be offered that is conditional upon the breed of the dog being handled.

Section 13. **Judges Book.** Each club holding Junior Showmanship shall provide for the judge a Judges Book which shall contain a separate sheet of the design prescribed by AKC for each Junior Showmanship class. The judge shall place the handlers First, Second, Third and Fourth and, after asking each placed handler to give his name, shall enter on the sheet the full names of the placed handlers, their armband numbers and the breeds of their dogs, and the total number of dogs competing in the class, and shall sign this book.

Section 14. **Limited Classes.** A club that is approved to hold a licensed or member all-breed show, may be approved to hold a Limited Junior Showmanship class or classes at its show, but no club will be approved to hold regular Junior Showmanship classes and Limited Junior Showmanship classes at the same show.

Limited Junior Showmanship classes shall be open only to Junior handlers who have qualified by reason of certain wins in Junior Showmanship competition as specified in the premium list, within a specified period of about 12 months ending not more than 3 months prior to the date of the show; and may be further limited to Junior handlers who reside within a specified geographical area, or who have qualified at shows held within a specified geographical area.

Section 15. **Exceptions for Limited Classes.** All of these Regulations relating to regular Junior Showmanship classes shall also apply to Limited Junior Showmanship classes except that:

(A) The club may choose to prepare an announcement, separate from the premium list, which shall give all of the required information on the Limited Junior Showmanship and which shall be distributed, on request, to eligible Junior handlers. Special entry forms, identification slips, and armbands, may also be provided, if necessary.

(B) The premium list or separate announcement may specify a closing date for acceptance of entries in Limited Junior Showmanship classes later than the date for closing of entries in the show.

(C) The dogs handled in Limited Junior Showmanship must be eligible for entry in Dog Shows or Obedience Trials. They may, but need not,

126

be entered in breed or obedience at the particular show. Any limitation or restriction on entries in a show shall not apply to dogs that are brought into the show premises only to be handled in Limited Junior Showmanship.

(D) The information on dogs to be handled in Limited Junior Showmanship that are not entered in the show, and the names of the Junior handlers, may but need not be given in the catalog.

(E) The age limits specified in Section 4 shall apply to the age of each Junior handler at the time of the last win required to qualify for the Limited Junior Showmanship class, rather than to the age on the date of the Limited Junior Showmanship competition.

(F) If the entries in Limited Junior Showmanship warrant, the club may specify, in the first or in a later announcement, that preliminary classes will be held at the show, from which the judge(s) will select a specified number of Juniors to compete for Best Junior Handler, and no placements will be made in the preliminary classes.

Section 16. **Records.** The Superintendent or Shows Secretary shall forward to the American Kennel Club, with the records of the show, the judge's books for the Junior Showmanship classes.

For those seeking further information, the address of the American Kennel Club is 51 Madison Avenue, New York, N.Y. 10010.

TRY   HARDER !

JUNIOR SHOWMANSHIP RECORD

Date	Show and Place	Dog's Name	Award	Remarks

Suggestion: If more space is needed, Xerox copies of this page, or use it as a model in drawing your own record forms.